THE
COACH'S
CRAFT

POWERFUL PRACTICES
TO SUPPORT SCHOOL LEADERS

KAY PSENCIK

Learning Forward
504 S. Locust St.
Oxford, OH 45056
513-523-6029
800-727-7288
Fax: 513-523-0638
Email: office@learningforward.org
www.learningforward.org

The Coach's Craft:
Powerful Practices to Support School Leaders
By Kay Psencik

Editor: Valerie von Frank
Copy editor: Sue Chevalier
Designer: Cheryl Addington
Cover design: Kitty Black
Project manager: Valerie von Frank

Printed in the United States of America
Item #B530

ISBN 978-1-936630-03-5

CONTENTS

ACKNOWLEDGMENTS

I am grateful for the learning opportunities I have had from Learning Forward over the past 30 years. I am especially grateful for the support of Stephanie Hirsh, executive director. I consider her a model learner, someone who is visionary, eager to grow and learn, and a continuous and fastidious promoter of professional learning as the most effective strategy for transforming schools and ensuring the success of all children.

I would like to thank Dave Ellis, president of The Brande Foundation; Dennis Sparks, emeritus executive director of the National Staff Development Council, now called Learning Forward; and Julio Olalla, president of Newfield Network, for their training and support which allowed me to develop competence and confidence as a coach.

And, of course, there is Valerie von Frank, the editor of this book. Somehow she made the book come alive, and I appreciate all that she has done. I also want to thank Sue Chevalier, whose attention to detail as copy editor ensured that the message would be heard without distraction, and Cheryl Addington, whose graphic design perfectly captures and supports the tone and message in a visual way.

I am grateful to my family for their love, care, and support. I come from a long line of strong women who believed that if we work hard and learn much, we will have whatever opportunities we want in life. I especially want to acknowledge my mother, Marjorie Ferrill, who is my continuous inspiration of how to work hard, love much, pray for and care for others, and live well. Furthermore, I have two wonderful daughters, Erin Psencik and Annette Jones, a supportive husband, Don, a handsome son-in-law, and two delightful granddaughters, Kate and Tory. When I think of them, I am energized to continue the work of transforming schools and developing strong, sustained leadership to ensure that all children have the opportunity to learn.

Most important, I want to thank the many principals and school leaders whose stories are told in this book. Though their real names are not used, their stories are real and the challenges they face every day would make most of us feel weak, ineffective, and even frightened. I am proud to have known each one, proud to have had the opportunity to serve them, and, most important, hopeful that by telling their stories in this book, others are inspired to develop their coaching craft so that every principal leads a community of learners who ensure the success of every child.

— *Kay Psencik*

"Skillful leadership on the part of principals and teachers
is essential if schools are to become communities
of learning for both students and educators. ...
Unfortunately, few principals and teachers have had
serious and sustained opportunities to cultivate the
skills associated with instructional leadership and the
building of professional communities."

— Sparks, 2002

As principals face higher expectations and greater educational needs, what strategies can they use that are most effective in helping them develop competence in their essential role of creating high-performing schools?

One of the essential strategies to support principals is to build their capacity to provide instructional leadership, according to a report by the National Association of Elementary School Principals (2008). "Principals must have time and resources to develop the knowledge and skills they need to lead high-performance schools, as well as the resources to function effectively as instructional leaders in their buildings."

Principals need visionary central support. Michael Fullan (2008) notes, "Investment in leadership development is important. Getting beyond resignation and the passive dependency that has been created by the prescriptions of the past 10 years requires a different kind of socialization for principals. In England, they have created the National College of School Leadership to develop leaders on a much larger scale. In District 2 in New York City, they deliberately built the capacity of principals through various processes such as intervisitations, during which principals developed deeper understanding not only of their own schools, but other schools as well."

Those in school districts responsible for principals must value principals' work — and value their learning. School leaders need in-depth, structured learning experiences, collaboration, and just-in-time professional learning. When district leaders focus on intense leadership development, they help leaders develop a shared vision around the district's mission and vision, as well as an understanding of how various innovations are designed to achieve those goals (Marzano & Waters, 2009). Through specialized institutes designed for deep learning and continuous follow-up and support, district leaders guide communities of principals to fully and successfully achieve the district's priorities. They support principals in establishing priority goals for themselves, and they work with principals to help them achieve those goals. When district leaders focus on leadership development, they provide and structure time for principals to work in teams to support one another, to solve problems, to develop strategies, and to engage in study. They organize strategies for principals to conduct structured walk-throughs in each other's schools, both for modeling and to share ideas with one another.

And when districts have an intense focus on leadership development, they ensure that each principal has a powerful coach who can mentor, model, question, encourage, and inspire — a coach who works side-by-side with the leader, inspiring the principal to focus on strengthening individual skills, to deepen his or her understanding of professional learning communities, and to develop the attitudes and aspirations needed for leading and learning.

All of these strategies are essential because principals, like all adult learners, learn best when the work matters to them at the moment. Adults have a deep need to be self-directing and learn best when they can set goals for themselves. Their readiness for learning increases when they have a specific need to know. Because all adults are social learners, they learn best when they collaborate with others. Their wealth of experiences both helps them learn and interferes in their ability to shape new directions for themselves. They tend, like all learners, to be more successful when they have an immediate application for what they are learning and effective strategies for reflecting (Knowles, 1989; Merriam & Caffarella, 1999; Brookfield, 1991).

As teams of principals work together to collaborate on efforts, observe each other working with staff, reflect on their practice, and study together, they accelerate their learning. When principals are coached, they develop confidence and competence as leaders around specific goals unique to their individual learning needs.

Coaching helped me shift my observations of the world, open myself up to new ways of thinking, see new possible actions, appreciate the present, and find wholeness.

Great coaching is an art. It involves skillfully asking questions and challenging assumptions. Coaching opens participants to changing the way they think about themselves, their leadership, and the opportunities they have to shape their own futures and the future of their schools. Coaching does not mean telling others what to do or how to solve their problems. It is not training. It is not being an empathetic friend. Coaching helps those being coached grow more confident and competent in leading and learning.

I coached a very successful, very experienced principal who had been transferred to a most challenging school. Not only had the school staff experienced turnover in leadership, but student achievement was so low that the state declared the school in need of restructuring. This principal had come from a very different setting, a magnet school program. Although he was tremendously committed to the children and his new school, he faced many challenges. As we began to visit, he shared his challenges with me and admitted he was discouraged by the lack of systems in the school. He was not sure he was always on the right track. Coaching renewed his confidence in his own ability to lead the school to higher performance.

Then there was a first-year principal in a difficult high school. Although she had been assistant principal in an elementary school for a year, she was not comfortable with or knowledgeable about life in a high school. When she first entered the school, she noticed a sign on the front office counter that said, "No change!" That was the unofficial school motto. The rumor was that if someone said, "We ought to …," then somebody else would issue a reminder, "No change! It says so in the office!"

This new principal hired a coach. Together, she and the coach set a goal that she would build powerful, purposeful relationships with staff and ensure that staff members clearly understood her values and vision for the school. The principal wanted to develop teacher leaders, and she wanted to guide the staff to develop a shared vision of higher achievement. With her coach, she designed a system of inquiry and a plan for gathering data about staff members' interests, needs, and aspirations. She practiced with her coach interactions she wanted to have with staff. She designed staff meetings to achieve her goal of shared leadership. As the school began to transform, teachers took the lead and began to value their learning. One teacher reported, "What I am learning is that I cannot solve problems by myself. When a problem arises, it takes a group of us to solve it. I think that is the key. ... To be successful, we had to come out of that seclusion, become a cohesive group, and work together."

Often principals have no coach to help them see the world differently, shape the school's direction, and resolve the issues they face. They find themselves in difficult situations and are expected to solve their problems alone. Sometimes they see no option but to find another position.

In the absence of a districtwide plan for principal development, coaching is essential. With a districtwide emphasis and focus on principal development, coaching contributes to principals' learning.

The art of great coaching

The great coaches of the world have unique and inspirational ways to lead others to find themselves, to discover their dreams and aspirations, and to generate the courage to achieve them. Those who aspire to be great coaches diligently seek to capture the art and science of this work.

I have had the wonderful gift not only of coaching many principals but of being coached myself. I was paired with a highly skilled coach. As I attended to the questions she asked and the challenges she posed, I grew in understanding and learned new ways of thinking. Where I saw barriers, she guided me in ways that helped me to envision a different future, to practice new skills, and to create purposeful, focused plans of action. She never advised or explained what I should do or how I should do it. She was a skilled questioner who guided me to find my own way using reflections that deepened my learning.

As my trust in my coach grew, I realized I could be myself with her. I could share my deepest fears, my most negative emotions, and all my attitudes without fear of being judged or exposed. When I was negative, she gently guided me back to my goals and vision. She laughed with me, celebrated my successes, and listened, listened, listened. I was always the center of her attention while she was coaching. Each conversation we had challenged my thinking and inspired me to work harder. Coaching helped me shift my observations of the world, open myself up to new ways of thinking, see new possible actions, appreciate the present, and find wholeness.

What are the skills of great coaches? What are their attitudes? How are they so courageous, inspirational, and challenging all at the same time? How do they inspire the passion of those they coach and lead them to achieve extraordinary goals?

Whether in the sports arena or guiding individuals to achieve their goals, coaches skillfully and precisely lead others to learning. The most successful coaches of principals understand themselves, the essential role they play, and the skills they need to have in order to inspire principals to lead communities where learning is the norm.

The purpose of this book is to nurture, support, and inspire those who coach principals to value their work and to develop their coaching skills. In addition, this book is meant to encourage principals to seek a coach to help facilitate their learning and transform their leadership.

To begin, I define coaching and distinguish mentoring, supervising, facilitating, life coaching, ontological coaching, and the values of these strategies in coaching principals. The book then is divided into three sections. Each section guides the reader into deeper thinking about the topic through story examples, a list of underlying assumptions, questions for reflection, and suggested new actions.

The first section focuses on the complexity of the principalship, the principal's role in building a high-achieving learning community, and principals' need for coaching. The second section describes the essential skills and character of effective coaches. These chapters explore the skills of an effective coach, social and emotional intelligence, physical and spiritual well-being, and wisdom. The final section focuses on strategies for effective coaching, such as developing listening skills; guiding principals to become observers; assessing observations as a basis for action; uncovering and challenging assumptions; asking good questions; developing a knowledge of good professional learning practices; helping principals use bodies, language, and emotions to open new possibilities; and working through high-stress situations.

By developing trust, using observation, employing laser-like listening and questioning skills, and sharing the benefit of their experience and wisdom, coaches guide those they coach to discover strengths, establish goals, and design strategies to achieve those goals. Coaches of principals have a unique opportunity to shape the very fabric of a school by developing a leader who affects staff and students, who shapes the culture where students and teachers work and learn together, and who benefits the community that surrounds the school.

The foundation of highly effective coaching

"Coaching is a practice that specializes in changing awareness, action, and the world around us. In systems language, this is called 'coevolution.' People change their environment, and their different experiences in this changed environment change their brains so that they make new changes. Coaching enables us to see this process at a new level and therefore to practice it more consciously than ever before."

— *Rock & Page, 2009*

"Knowledge is the rediscovery of our own insights."

— *Plato*

In a meeting with a group of editors, authors, and other publishers, the head of a large publishing corporation told the group that when he took over as chief executive officer of his organization, he had a hard time understanding the world in which he found himself. His background to that point had not involved finance. He said he spent most of his time analyzing the company's financial challenges, studying how resources were being used, researching new publishing technology, and reviewing how the company's revenues aligned with its goals.

Finally, realizing that he couldn't be the leader he wanted to be if all his attention was focused on this single aspect of the business, he found a coach. He said the coach asked precise questions and challenged his assessments, and he soon found himself thinking about the company differently. He began to appreciate the complexity and challenges of publishing in a multimedia world. He began to see beyond the finances to new ways to become a visionary leader.

In schools, many principals have succeeded by developing strong managerial skills. They likely have taken the traditional route, becoming an assistant principal for discipline for several years as preparation for the principalship. As they approach the lead job, they are certain that if they cannot *manage* the building, their tenure will be short-lived. They make sure every classroom has a teacher in it for the day and that students are successfully loaded on buses at the end of that day. They learn these management skills on the job, over time, and through experience.

Most principals find that management issues, simply opening the doors each day and ensuring that school runs smoothly and safely, can fill their day. However, as pressures increase on schools to produce more high-achieving students, effective leadership entails a broader vision, and trial by fire is an ineffective and inefficient path to success.

What principals think, say, and do matters for student and staff learning (Sparks, 2002; Waters, Marzano, & McNulty, 2003; NAESP, 2008). When principals develop specific skills and attitudes, they lead others to engage in powerful professional learning. When they use student data to drive decisions, develop a shared vision with faculty, instill learning as a norm for adults and students, establish clear plans of action, and monitor their efforts, student achievement in their schools increases (Hord & Sommers, 2008). Although research around the skills of highly effective principals is often shared in principal certification programs, those enrolled in certification programs generally lack opportunities to practice the skills immediately in meaningful, authentic ways. In certification programs, future principals learn *about* leading schools and *about* leadership. The challenge is that they learn how to be effective only while on the job.

What if principals had coaches to help them in the challenging role of leading schools?

Does coaching matter?

To break the barriers of outdated modes of leadership, principals need a new vision of school leadership, a clear understanding of the role and responsibilities of a highly effective principal, and coaches who help them develop and hone their skills.

As principals face greater demands and pressure to have all students reach higher levels of achievement, leading is increasingly challenging. Leadership requires continual learning and a cycle of improvement, with staff continually exploring and honing new skills. However, the traditional model of school leadership, in which principals are not skilled in leading professional learning, is pervasive. The leader's role is pivotal to schools becoming communities of learners in which teachers continuously improve their practice so they can enable students to succeed at higher levels.

The research both on coaching executives and
on coaching teachers indicates that coaching
makes a difference for those who are coached.

While coaches, clients, and other professionals who use coaching strategies and
skills attest that coaching works, little scientific evidence exists to support the efficacy
of coaching. More organizations now are beginning to explore the impact of coaching
on executives in implementing change.

Anthony M. Grant, Linley Curtaynes, and Geraldine Burton (2009) conducted a
randomized controlled study of 41 executives in a public health agency. The executives
received 360-degree feedback, a half-day leadership workshop, and four individual
coaching sessions over 10 weeks. Compared with a control group, those who were
coached were more likely to achieve their goals, showed increased resilience and workplace well-being, and demonstrated reduced depression and stress. Participants found
coaching helped increase their self-confidence and personal insight, built management
skills, and helped them deal with organizational change. Findings indicate that short-
term coaching can be effective and that evidence-based executive coaching can help
people deal with the uncertainty and challenges inherent in organizational change.

A similar study conducted by Frode Moen, Einar Skaalvik, and Colleen Hacker
(2009) explored the effects of an executive coaching program on performance.
Coaches worked with 144 executives and middle managers from a Fortune 500 high-
tech company for a year. The findings indicate that coaching had significant effects
on psychological variables such as self-efficacy, goal setting, sense of control over one's
success, and job satisfaction, all of which affect job performance.

In the education field, studies have focused on coaching teachers. Far West
Laboratory (1984) presented findings from a five-year longitudinal study beginning
in 1979 that showed that coaching teachers made a significant difference in teacher
effectiveness. A research team studied approximately 80 schools in 20 California
districts and examined whether peer coaching increased teachers' implementation of
new skills. "The research team found that when teachers were given only a description
of new instructional skills, only 10% used the skill in the classroom. When each of the
next three components of peer coaching — modeling, practice, and feedback — were
added to the training, teachers' implementation of the teaching skill increased by 2%
to 3% each time a new component was added to the training process. Description,

modeling, practice, and feedback resulted in a 16% to 19% transfer of skill to class-room use. However, when coaching was added to the staff development, approximately 95% of the teachers implemented the new skills in their classrooms" (Cornett & Knight, 2008, pp. 196-197).

The research both on coaching executives and on coaching teachers indicates that coaching makes a difference for those who are coached.

Coaching, then, may hold the key to deepening leaders' understanding, wisdom, skills, behaviors, attitudes, and aspirations, helping them to create and lead high-performing organizations. Coaching unlocks an individual's natural leadership potential and helps that person become his or her best self. Through coaching, school leaders learn to see new opportunities for themselves and others, and they become true leaders.

Coaches for principals

Districts often don't assign principals coaches because educators lack a clear vision of the power of coaching to help principals gain skills. Terms such as supervising, mentoring, and inducting generally are used to describe how newly assigned principals learn districts' policies and procedures. Even accepted terms for coaching leaders vary — including executive coaching, cognitive coaching, transformational coaching, life coaching, organizational coaching, and ontological coaching. The definitions and distinctions of each of these forms may add to the confusion about coaching's value and purpose, and about its connection to leading schools to high performance levels.

In addition, those responsible for principals may hold an unstated belief that lead-ers should know what to do — that hiring the right person by definition means that the person is skilled. Some have the perspective that school leaders' credibility comes from their role authority, and they therefore do not or should not need assistance or coaching. Of course, hiring the right person to be principal is fundamental to school success. No amount of coaching can overcome a person in the wrong job (Marzano & Waters, 2009). However, once the best person is hired, the way to ensure that person's success is to support his or her ongoing learning.

Another challenge is an insufficient number of skilled coaches able to offer principals strategic support. While executive coaching and coaching for business CEOs is a well-organized and highly respected field, coaching for principals is not as advanced in having agreed-upon processes and structures to help principals develop specific skills.

Although the nation has developed an intense focus on instructional coaching and teacher leadership, which are essential to teacher learning, leadership development and principal coaching have received less attention. Yet, whether teacher leadership flourishes depends a great deal on the principal's leadership vision, skills, styles, and attitudes (Hirsh & Killion, 2007; Hord & Sommers, 2008).

ASSUMPTIONS

» Principals who have effective coaches are more successful than those who do not.

» Effective coaching leads principals to develop the understanding, skills, behaviors, attitudes, and aspirations essential to increase student and staff learning.

Effective coaching

Coaches who improve a principal's learning understand the role, skills, and dispositions of highly effective principals. Coaches have conversations with those they are coaching that go beyond short-term goals and explore the person's life, dreams, and hopes. The coach is skilled at listening and questioning to allow leaders to unlock their potential and discover new pathways. The coach works continuously to earn the trust of those being coached so that principals are comfortable sharing leadership issues.

Coaches who are most effective with principals have had similar leadership positions and been responsible for raising student performance. They know the joys and difficulties of the work. While they have had similar experiences, they do not assume that their experiences are the same as the experiences of those they coach. They understand adult learners, the importance of building trust, and how observations of the world either open opportunities or close doors. Skillful coaches know what skills principals need in order to be successful and can artfully and precisely model these skills. They have the strengths of listening and questioning, and they have sufficient strategies to help principals develop these skills. In addition to the skills of life coaches and ontological coaches, effective coaches are grounded in change theory, the structure of the professional learning community, and strategies for transforming schools (Hirsh & Killion, 2007; Hord & Sommers, 2008). Coaches of principals need an array of strategies and tools, a clear vision of the coaching role, a passion for learning, and the courage to ask challenging questions.

Coaches help principals lead. They help principals develop essential job skills and apply these skills systematically and purposefully in the principals' daily efforts to lead. Quality coaches inspire and energize those they coach. Through questioning and challenging a leader's assumptions, a quality coach guides the principal to see new possibilities for the principal personally and for those the principal leads. Quality coaching helps leaders change behaviors, build confidence, and find courage.

A definition, rationale, and Innovation Configuration

An Innovation Configuration is an established and well-researched format. The idea was developed by experts in a national research center studying educational change (Hall & Hord, 2010; Hord, Rutherford, Huling-Austin, & Hall, 1987). An IC identifies and describes the major components of a new practice and describes various uses along a continuum, ranging from ideal implementation to nonuse.

Figure 1.1 is an Innovation Configuration for coaching principals based on the essential components of coaching. Coaches can use an Innovation Configuration (IC) in many ways, including using it to identify their strengths and weaknesses by finding the description that best matches their skill level. The IC can be used to set goals for strengthening skills and, most importantly, to help coaches realize the complexity of their work and the commitment needed to be effective.

Aspiring coaches can use this IC to determine where they are on the continuum and refer frequently to it to deepen their understanding of the coach's role as they work through the strategies in subsequent chapters in this book.

FIGURE 1.1 Innovation Configuration for a highly effective coach

Definition

Coaches who improve a principal's learning understand the role, skills, and dispositions of highly effective principals. Coaches have conversations with those they coach that go beyond short-term goals and explore the leader's life, dreams, and hopes. The coach is skilled at listening and questioning to allow leaders to unlock their potential and discover new pathways. The coach works continuously to earn the leader's trust so that the leader is comfortable sharing leadership issues.

Rationale

To break through the barriers of outdated modes of leadership, principals need a new vision of school leadership, a clear understanding of the roles and responsibilities of highly effective principals, and coaches who help them develop and hone their skills.

As principals face greater demands and pressure to increase all students' success, leading is increasingly challenging. The traditional model of school leadership, in which principals are not skilled in leading professional learning, is pervasive. The leader's role is pivotal to schools becoming communities of learners in which teachers continuously improve their practice so they can enable students to succeed at higher levels.

Quality coaches inspire and energize those they coach. Through questioning and challenging the leader's assumptions, a quality coach guides the principal in seeing new possibilities for the principal and those he or she leads. Quality coaching helps leaders change behaviors, build confidence, and find courage.

Desired outcome I:	The coach builds a safe and nurturing environment in which those being coached are comfortable sharing work challenges, establishing strategies for building shared vision in their schools, and implementing purposeful innovations.
Desired outcome II:	The coach structures the learning to ensure that leaders develop knowledge and the skills to create and lead learning communities in which all students and staff are learning.
Desired outcome III:	The coach continuously learns in order to improve.

FIGURE 1.1 Innovation Configuration for a highly effective coach

Desired outcome I: The coach builds a safe and nurturing environment in which those being coached are comfortable sharing work challenges, establishing strategies for building shared vision in their schools, and implementing purposeful innovations.

Level 1	Level 2	Level 3	Level 4	Level 5
The coach is a trusted confidante of the coachee.	The coach is trusted by the coachee.	Though the coach talks about the importance of trust in the relationship, the coachee is not comfortable being open and honest in coaching sessions.	The coach assumes trust in the relationship but does not intentionally focus on building a trusting relationship with the coachee.	The coach violates trust and places the coachee at risk.
The coach has high regard for the coachee's emotional safety and security.	The coach is conscious of being a model for the coachee and skillfully prepares for coaching sessions to ensure the coachee maintains a sense of wellness.	The coach understands and uses skills with the coachee that reflect adult learning styles; however, the coach has little understanding of a theory of change that would guide the learner to new leadership skills.	Coaching sessions are activity- and incident-driven and focus on problem solving. Little emphasis is placed on learning new skills, developing new attitudes, or exploring the coachee's deeply rooted assumptions that may be holding him or her back.	The coach is more concerned about his or her own well-being and sees coaching as a way to increase his or her own confidence, power, and financial security.
The coach is conscious of his or her own intentions, and the coachee sees congruence between verbal and nonverbal cues.	The coach understands that all adults have unique learning styles and designs coaching sessions to best meet the coachee's needs.			The coach often lets his or her personal concerns and personal stories enter into the conversation during coaching sessions.
The coach has a deep understanding of individual and organizational change and is grounded in the principles of systems thinking and adult learning.	The coach has achieved success as a school leader and systems thinker.			
The coach maintains a high regard for the coachee at all times. Both coach and coachee are clear about their own values, philosophies, emotional and social well-being.	The coach has the coachee's best interests in mind at all times.			

FIGURE 1.1 Innovation Configuration for a highly effective coach

Desired outcome II: The coach structures the learning to ensure that leaders develop knowledge and the skills to create and lead learning communities in which all students and staff are learning.

Level 1	Level 2	Level 3	Level 4	Level 5
The coach uses a variety of modeling, mediating, visioning, and inquiry strategies to help the coachee understand communities, their dynamics and interactions, and their need for purpose and learning. The coach skillfully selects learning strategies and goal-setting systems that best meet the coachee's needs. The coach is grounded in the definition, standards, principles, and practices of professional learning.	The coach uses research and inquiry skills to help the coachee understand the characteristics of a professional learning community. The coach focuses the coachee on learning new skills, new attitudes, and new behaviors so that he or she is open to new possibilities and sets meaningful, challenging goals.	The coach uses questioning strategies skillfully in working with the coachee. The coach helps the coachee communicate and clarify goals and personal expectations but struggles to model or design effective learning strategies for the coachee.	The coach uses storytelling and questioning strategies that leave the coachee dwelling on issues and blaming others for the situation. The coach, unclear about the characteristics of a professional learning community, uses incident-focused, problem-solving strategies that do not build vision.	The coach listens to the coachee's stories but is unclear when to interject questions that might lead to learning. The coach is not familiar with the characteristics of a professional learning community, leaving the coachee to take whatever direction seems best at the time.

FIGURE 1.1 Innovation Configuration for a highly effective coach

Desired outcome III: The coach continuously learns in order to improve.

Level 1	Level 2	Level 3	Level 4	Level 5
The coach routinely self-assesses and regularly learns new and effective strategies for coaching. The coach works collaboratively with other coaches to strengthen his or her skills and to reflect on the impact coaching is having. The coach regularly sets goals for himself or herself to use new skills and strategies. He or she seeks a coach to facilitate his or her learning and to monitor his or her own progress. The coach consistently uses the coachee's feedback about coaching's effect on the coachee's learning. The coach modifies his or her approach based on that learning.	The coach is continuously learning new and effective strategies for coaching principals. The coach regularly discusses with other coaches what they are learning and experiencing. The coach regularly sets personal goals to increase his or her effectiveness. The coach seeks the coachee's feedback about his or her effectiveness in developing the coachee's competence to lead professional learning communities.	The coach attends conferences and sessions on becoming an effective coach and stays current in the thinking, skills, and research around coaching principals. The coach rarely discusses with others what the coach is learning. The coach rarely if ever sets goals for himself or herself to increase his or her effectiveness. The coach seeks feedback from coachees about his or her effectiveness.	The coach views himself or herself as a learner, but is confident she or he has effective strategies for coaching principals. The coach seeks general feedback from the coachee but rarely seeks sufficient or precise feedback in order to identify specific strengths and weaknesses in his or her coaching work that can help guide a learning plan.	The coach is confident in his or her coaching and relies on past learning to hone the coachee's skills.

REFLECTIONS

An important attribute of the learning coach is personal reflection. Take time to reflect on the following prompts. Write your responses in the book or in your learning journal.

The values that guide my actions in coaching others:

My beliefs about learning:

My purpose in coaching principals:

My hopes and aspirations for those I coach:

The things I need to learn to be more effective as a coach:

STRATEGIES AND INVESTIGATIONS

» Reflect on your experiences coaching others. Make notes. What skills, attitudes, and strategies seem to be most effective? What challenges do you face regularly?

» Use the Innovation Configuration and the self-assessment tool in Appendix A to think deeply about yourself as a coach. What observations can you make about yourself in the role? What might you need to learn?

» Using the Innovation Configuration, determine your strengths as a coach. What contributes to your strengths? Describe them. Think of evidence that you have to support your thinking. How can you capitalize on your strengths to be more effective when coaching principals?

» List the ideas in this chapter that most intrigued you or caused you to think more deeply about your coaching. Where could you learn more about those ideas?

» Begin a journal to reflect on strategies, skills, behaviors, and attitudes as you grow as a coach. Start your journal with a restatement of your philosophy about learning and coaching, including your purpose in coaching principals and the values that ground your actions. Record what you learn about yourself and about coaching. Keep one section for recording questions. Refer to your writing often as your thinking becomes clearer. My model philosophy about learning and coaching appears in Appendix B, but you may have a more compelling philosophy and begin without referencing it.

» Using the effective coach's self-assessment in Appendix A, establish a goal(s) that builds on your strengths and addresses an area of concern. Often when we build on our strengths, we diminish our weaknesses.

» Establish a community of coaches who will support and learn from one another. Establish norms and protocols for working together that honor the privacy of those being coached. Design a structure that allows members to problem solve and talk about coaching, while also coaching each other and getting feedback. (See a protocol for designing protocols, a protocol for establishing norms, and a protocol for structured feedback sessions with other coaches in Appendix C.)

RESOURCES FOR CHAPTER 1

Bloom, G., Castagna, C., Moir, E., & Warren, B. (2005). *Blended coaching: Skills and strategies to support principal development.* Thousand Oaks, CA: Corwin Press.

Edwards, J.L. (2008). *Cognitive coaching: A synthesis of the research.* Highland Ranch, CO: Center for Cognitive Coaching.

Fielden, S. (2005). *Literature review: Coaching effectiveness — a summary.* London: NHS Leadership Centre.

Killion, J. & Harrison, C. (2006). *Taking the lead: New roles for teachers and school-based coaches.* Oxford, OH: NSDC.

Knight, J. (2009). *Coaching approaches & perspectives.* Thousand Oaks, CA: Corwin Press.

Mizell, H. (2001, Summer). How to get there from here. *Journal of Staff Development, 22*(3), 18-20.

Stoker, D.R. (2005). Approaches to research on executive and organizational coaching outcomes. *International Journal of Coaching in Organizations, 3*(1), 6-13.

Wasylyshyn, K. (2003). Executive coaching: An outcome study. *Consulting Psychology Journal: Practice & Research, 55*(2), 94-106.

"Many years ago, I adopted this credo: Always strive to
be a better you. Its origins sprout from the ancient Greek
philosophy of paideia, which espouses the belief that life's
true goal is to attain one's ultimate potential. The nifty twist
is the idea that rides shotgun: The closer one approaches,
the more one's ultimate potential expands. Thus, the result is
the pursuit of an ever-elusive quarry, the constant challenge
to obtain the unattainable."

— Hall, 2005

The facilitator had already begun an administrative session on strategic
planning when one of the principals came in late. This principal sat down
quickly, but he didn't join in the group work. He repeatedly leaned back
in his chair and chuckled to himself, then appeared deep in thought. His
actions became so distracting that the facilitator finally asked, "What's
so funny?"

"Four pieces of chicken!" the principal said. "Four pieces of chicken! This
district says it wants me to be an instructional leader. They've given me a lot
of leadership training. I *know* what I need to do. But I keep being sidetracked
by the four-pieces-of-chicken factor.

"I spent the last two days tracking down what happened to four pieces of chicken that went missing from the cafeteria," he continued. "The cafeteria manager was furious about this alleged theft. I tried to tell her, 'It's only four pieces of chicken. Maybe a student was hungry and took extra.' But she wanted a full investigation. The staff got angry at me for not taking the incident more seriously, so I ended up spending hours interviewing anyone who might have seen the heinous act. I talked to all the students who were in the cafeteria at the time until, finally, two boys admitted, 'We were really hungry! We're sorry; we'll pay for the chicken!' You see, it's really all just about four pieces of chicken."

A complex job

Few jobs present as many challenges to an individual's intelligence, problem solving, and emotions as the principalship. An effective principal masters a broad spectrum of educational and management challenges. Principals deal with literally hundreds of brief tasks each day, sometimes 50 to 60 separate interactions in an hour (Peterson, 1982, 1998). Any given hour, for example, may bring the challenge of a classroom without a teacher, a child's broken arm, a student scuffle, a request from the central office for data, and myriad other requests for information from parents, students, and teachers. Not only are there immediate challenges in the school, but principals also are responsible for ensuring improved student performance.

Effective principals build shared vision, facilitate collaboration, develop others' leadership skills, and build and maintain relationships with multiple communities. In addition, they lead change processes in often highly politicized and conservative institutions. It is no wonder we are facing a shortage of leaders.

Research indicates the population of principals is aging, and we lack an adequate pool of candidates to replace them. A RAND study (Gates, Ringel, Santibanez, Ross, & Chung, 2003) found that the nation's principals, like its teachers, are growing older as a group. From 1988 to 2000, the average age of principals increased from 47.8 to 49.3 in the public sector and from 46 to 49.9 in the private sector. The age at which candidates become principals also has shifted dramatically. In 1988, 38% of new public school principals (i.e., those with three or fewer years of experience as a principal) were 40 or younger; by 2000, the figure was 12%. For new private school principals, the shift was similar. At the same time, the U.S. Department of Labor's Bureau of Labor Statistics (n.d.) estimates that the need for educational administrators will grow 8% between 2008 and 2018.

A trend in principal candidates shows an increase in candidates for the principalship who lack deep grounding in teaching. In addition, although preservice certification programs give new administrators some grounding, these programs are not designed to provide support when inexperienced principals begin their work (Bloom,

In reality, as with teaching, the real learning begins when the new principal walks into the building.

Castagna, Moir, & Warren, 2005). In reality, as with teaching, the real learning begins when the new principal walks into the building.

When districts are able to find qualified candidates, many do not remain in the job. Most leaders who leave cite reasons more related to their own emotional intelligence than to their knowledge of reading programs or their ability to construct a master schedule (Goleman, 1998).

To accelerate principal learning, districts can ensure that each principal, regardless of years of experience, has a coach. However, those who coach principals have a responsibility to understand the complexity of the school leader's work. Consider these true stories from principals' lives.

A skilled instructional coach had spent years supporting her colleagues and was highly respected for her expertise in the school where she coached. When the school's principal left, the superintendent recommended the coach for the job, saying she was a natural fit and a strong instructional leader. But teachers who had respected the coach for her instructional expertise as a peer had difficulty with her as a principal. They constantly grieved her actions through the teachers association. The district became embroiled in legal issues. Then the superintendent accepted a job in another district, a new superintendent was hired, and in less than six months, the beginning principal was asked to look for a job in another district. She was surprised, unprepared, and devastated. Her coach asked her strategic questions to help her plan for leaving with honor and a vision for her own future.

Not only do principals deal with hundreds of decisions, focus on developing learning communities in a culture that nurtures learning, manage staff energy, build consensus, and hold high expectations to facilitate change, but they must be accountable to the public and to staff (Marzano, Waters, & McNulty, 2005).

In another district, the superintendent promised the interim principal of a large high school that she would name him principal at an upcoming board meeting. However, staff saw the interim principal as the superintendent's "yes man" and began to voice dissatisfaction to the press, school board members, fellow staff members, and even students. Then an incident occurred. Not recognizing the importance of a bell awarded to the school in a competition against another high school in the region, the interim principal stored it. The entire community was up in arms. The issue became so publicized, including in the local media, that the interim was moved and stowed away in the central office.

The interim principal's coach began strategic questioning to help him analyze the events, make sense of them, accept responsibility for the outcomes, and determine a plan of action to facilitate a smooth transition between principals. Once the interim had a clear understanding and could articulate his learning, the coach began to help him consider revised career goals.

Terrence Deal and Kent Peterson (1998) state that principals must focus not only on the immediate incidents that consume their time, but must work to shape the professional culture. If the challenges of shaping a learning culture are not addressed, the school culture may turn toxic. Toxic cultures often result when principals do not uncover the school's "hidden history."

All the principals in a large suburban district respected one particular principal for his long-term commitment to one school. Major demographic shifts in his student population and growth in the school population over several years concerned the teachers, who were unsure how best to meet the needs of incoming students. The teachers were not as successful with this population as with past students. In addition, new parents and students did not feel welcome in the school and were beginning to distrust the school staff. The principal worked longer and longer hours, trying to build a relationship with these disillusioned parents. Not realizing the extent to which his health was suffering, he did not feel he had time to go to the doctor until he collapsed and was hospitalized with pneumonia.

Once his health was restored, the principal began sessions with a coach about how to succeed while maintaining a healthy lifestyle. He created a plan of action for himself and asked for coaching to address the underlying issue: students and staff not finding success.

Principals, as middle managers, have a difficult position within the organization. When they successfully lead their schools to raise student performance, they often work long hours, are disconnected from their families, feel isolated, and are overwhelmed by responsibilities. They may work with little support from peers or their

> The coach supports, inspires, and encourages
> principals to achieve their goals and is an essential
> part of an effective theory of change focused on
> principal professional learning.

superintendents. Extra and cocurricular activities can consume their time, erode their ability to be strong instructional leaders, and drain their energy. Students with a range of needs, and the rules and innovations imposed by outside agencies and district-level administrators, often leave school leaders feeling less than effective.

Yet principals seldom have opportunities to collaborate with other principals or to be coached. The person in the school responsible for ensuring that staff and students learn is given little if any support to grow as a learner and to succeed at leading the school to a higher level of performance. Some principals resort to simply managing the building and keeping as many people happy as possible. Their primary learning strategies are reading before they drop off to sleep or attending conferences to escape the continuous whitewater of school life.

Districts' responsibility for leader learning

While many districts focus extensive resources on teachers' professional development, district leaders may assume that principals do not need additional support because they have the skills to implement innovations, or that the principal can rely on teachers' understanding from *their* professional learning about a program or strategy. They may assume that, having hired the best possible person, that individual has the knowledge he or she needs to be successful.

A high school principal was respected by her peers for her leadership; however, she felt isolated in her role. When a position opened in central office, she decided to propose to her superintendent that the position be redesigned to include coaching to help develop principals' leadership. She carefully researched her plan and made her presentation. Though the superintendent was supportive, others in the administrative cabinet were not. They reasoned, "We hire good people to lead our schools; they know what to do. If they don't, they should not be principals." The idea was tabled indefinitely.

Coaching, however, can make a difference. Just as with teachers, coaching provides precise support. The coach supports, inspires, and encourages principals to achieve their goals and is an essential part of an effective theory of change focused on principal professional learning.

A new high school principal was reviewing student data and observing staff. He wanted to help teachers develop a shared vision and form a professional learning community. He established a leadership team and discussed his observations of the school. He engaged teachers in a conversation about their own observations and what they believed was possible. The staff read several books together, including *Leading Professional Learning Communities* (Corwin Press, 2008). They researched highly effective high schools, clarified their assumption that all students could be internationally competitive, and described their school as they wished it to be, answering: What would our curriculum standards and curriculum look like? What would students be doing? What are the most effective ways to assess student learning on international standards? What great performances or projects would students need to be doing? What do teachers do in a high-achieving school? How are parents involved?

At first, some staff members were skeptical. Some were sarcastic. Others wanted to stand back and observe. The new principal encouraged everyone to participate. The leadership team began to use technology to explore, study, and share ideas. Team members surveyed local industries to see what industry leaders wanted in employees. They studied the research and ideas behind the Partnership for 21st Century Skills, a national organization that advocates for 21st-century readiness for every student. They put their work on shared drives so everyone could see what was being learned. They got ideas from student focus groups. Still, they were not finished. They worked with the full faculty, students, and parents over the year to develop a vision, and everyone's energy, optimism, and enthusiasm grew.

Then the superintendent mandated a uniform approach to instruction at all the schools, requiring that teachers districtwide use the same instructional strategies. Learning clubs across the district would study the same strategies in a three-year initiative. Although the superintendent's program had merit, the high school staff was angry and resentful. Teachers were being diverted from their shared vision based on their own research to an innovation they had no part in selecting.

The principal called on his coach, who guided him to reflect on how his own attitude was stirring significant anger among the staff. He and the coach explored alternate views and began to think of how to integrate the mandated approach into the work teachers had already done. With coaching, the principal smartly and quickly became more optimistic and began to challenge teachers to think about how the superintendent's innovation could benefit the school. Without coaching, he likely would have been stuck in his view: "Why did we do all that work? We have no control over decisions!"

Principals are expected to ensure every student's success, manage facilities and staffs, implement district innovations, and keep multiple constituencies happy. A principal might find the district is simultaneously changing curriculum in several content areas; purchasing new materials for multiple content areas; implementing new and challenging instructional strategies such as differentiated instruction; using technology and inquiry through the curriculum; designing quarterly assessments for all schools to use; establishing strategies for Response to Intervention; and even more — leaving the principal to incorporate all of these into a school work plan and implement the ideas successfully and quickly. As Michael Fullan (2001) says, leadership is a complex art. The need for support to develop the skills necessary to be effective in the face of such complexity is great.

A theory of change

How do principals best learn and grow? A theory of change can help central office staff, staff developers, and especially coaches support principals in reaching higher levels of professional learning. A theory of change is a process of thinking through what it will take to achieve a vision or goal.

One simple theory of change is:

Figure 2.1 is an example of a theory of change that leads to principals learning. The example is grounded in Dennis Sparks' work (2002). This theory of change requires district-level involvement in examining assumptions about principal learning.

As principals and those who facilitate their learning articulate the behaviors, attitudes, and skills principals need in order to do well, they set targets for self-assessment, goals, and portfolios that reflect their learning. They rely for learning and intervention on intensive academies, peer partners, study teams, and coaching. These systems of building a community of learners among principals allow principals to work together, study together, observe one another, and give each other feedback. The principals commit not only to their own growth but begin to see they are essential to the learning of their peers. A community is vital to principals being able to thrive.

Coaching also is vital to principals' success. Coaching provides just-in-time, personalized support that every principal needs regardless of years of experience. Through skillful coaching, principals continuously explore how what they are learning in sessions and in small groups applies to them and their schools. The coach helps the principal solve individual problems and face challenging issues that the principal may not want to share with anyone else.

Here are the essential elements of this theory.

1. Articulate the skills, disposition, and behaviors of effective principals. All in the organization need a common understanding of the essential skills, dispositions, and behaviors of highly effective principals. District leadership teams should sort through the plethora of skill lists in the research to determine what is essential to the district's context and develop statements such as: "In this district, our principals will ..." Too many skills can be overwhelming.

FIGURE 2.1 A theory of change for principal growth

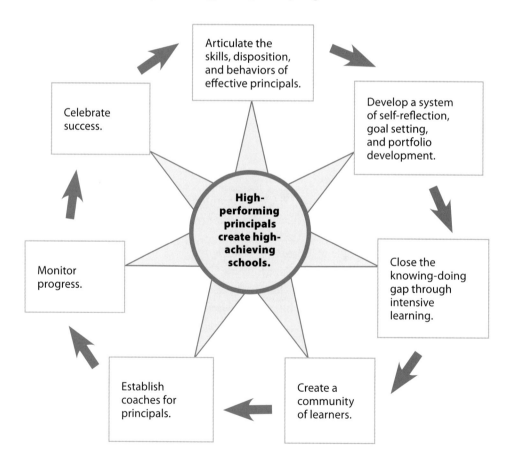

"What new behaviors am I using in school? What effect are those behaviors having on teacher practice? What are the results in student learning?"

In an internal district initiative, the Austin Independent School District administration, for example, established that principals should: 1) lead learning; 2) establish, articulate, and implement the vision of the school in relationship to the district's vision; 3) create an atmosphere of openness and mutual trust that fosters engagement of others; 4) support parents in assuming responsibility for their children's educational achievement; 5) establish an environment for creative and active school community participation with purpose and focus; 6) forge effective parent and community partnerships which support the achievement of every child; 7) value and respect diversity as a strength; 8) leverage, expand, and increase resources and capacity; and 9) enjoy and celebrate the journey. These essential areas were the basis of planning all professional learning for district administrators.

In another example, the Ohio leadership framework identifies six skill areas: data and decision making, focused goal setting, instruction and learning, community engagement, resource management, and board development and governance. Within each area, the state department of education identified the essential practices of central office staff and school leaders (Ohio Leadership Advisory Council, 2008).

The point of clarifying essential skills is to build shared understanding of what behaviors are essential for principals and the standards to be used for principals learning.

2. Develop a system of self-reflection, goal setting, and portfolio development.
Once the critical skills have been articulated, principals assess their effectiveness. They may use focus groups with their own staff, students, parents, and community members or use perception inventories to determine what others think of their leadership. They also may use tools such as the change facilitator's survey (Hall & Hord, 2010) or a tool of their own that focuses on the list of skills essential for them to practice effectively. Using such tools helps principals consider others' perspectives. When principals have a clear assessment of their own strengths and weaknesses, they are ready to set challenging goals for themselves. While principals often have set professional goals, those goals rarely have been grounded in an articulated set of essential skills.

The identified skills can be used to create a self-assessment tool as a basis for coaching. A sample principal self-assessment appears in Appendix A. Principals and coaches can use conversations about these skills to guide the principal to achieve goals. Once the goals are clearly articulated, principals who achieve them establish their own theory of change, determine logical innovations and interventions, and design a results-oriented plan of action.

3.   Close the knowing-doing gap through intensive learning. The third component of this model theory of change is opportunity for deep learning experiences through intensive academies. Because of the complex nature of school leadership, few principals spend thoughtful time on one topic. A principal rarely has extensive time to understand how to build trust in a school, for example, or to study strategies to create effective collaboration. Intensive study in academy settings gives principals the opportunity to slow down, be reflective, and figure out how to apply concepts to their own schools.

4.   Create a community of learners. Under current assumptions and practices, principals work in isolation. As districts build communities of principals who support each other, principals grow to see greater possibilities for themselves and create innovative ways to support one another on their learning journey, accelerating learning for all.

5.   Establish coaches for principals. Coaching principals can help leaders learn to change behavior and to develop new skills and attitudes, regardless of the district's additional learning strategies. Other strategies for principal learning, if implemented effectively, provide frameworks and directions for goal setting and ways to facilitate learning, but without coaching, they are insufficient and likely will fail to lead to principals learning new skills. Attending conferences, institutes, and summer leadership academies has not led to dramatic changes in principals' behavior. Coaching is a significant factor in any theory of change for principal development.

6.   Monitor progress. Establishing measures of effectiveness is vital. Portfolios may help assess impact, along with inventories of teachers' perceptions, observations in the school, and student performance data. By using a variety of tools, principals begin to determine their progress in learning new skills and adopting new behaviors. Using the same or similar tools that they used to determine their goal, they note advances in their leadership development. They ask and answer the question, "What new behaviors am I using in school? What effect are those behaviors having on teacher practice? What are the results in student learning?"

7.   Celebrate success. Celebrations are essential for creating energy to prompt principals to set even more challenging goals for themselves and to feel confident they can achieve them. Through public sharing of accomplishments, learning, the impact of the work, and next goals, principals celebrate learning, engage in a cycle of continuous learning, and send the message, "I am a learner and a leader; I make a difference in my school." Celebration and public sharing really bring the process back to the start and the questions in the first component: What do we know now that we did not know before? What did we do that increased our own learning? What challenges are we still facing? What goals do we need to set for ourselves now? The cycle begins again.

Developing a theory of change

Developing a theory of change involves backward mapping and considering not only what steps to take, but also exploring potential barriers to achieving the goal. Developing a theory of change involves five stages:

1. Identify a long-term goal and the assumptions behind it.
2. Create a backward map, considering preconditions as well as requirements for achieving the goal.
3. Identify the interventions essential to create the designed change.
4. Develop measures of effectiveness.
5. Write a narrative to explain the logic behind the goal and innovation.

An effective way to begin creating a theory of change is to establish a district team of administrators and teachers charged with writing one. Most understand that change is challenging and people naturally resist, but they have not really studied ways to overcome these barriers. When leaders deepen their understanding of change processes

ASSUMPTIONS

» A principal's daily life is complex and challenging.

» Principals accelerate their learning when they engage in meaningful conversation with other principals and with their coach.

» Districts that value professional learning for principals incorporate coaching into their theory of change.

» Coaching provides just-in-time professional learning for principals to inspire school leaders to view matters with a fresh perspective, creating possibilities for them.

and organizational change, they are able to make thoughtful decisions about principal professional learning. A district leadership team may begin the work by hosting focus groups or open forums with principals to listen to their perspectives and to ask, "What are your needs?" and "What skills do you believe are essential for you to develop?" The leadership team should study and understand Learning Forward's definition of quality professional learning, the Standards for Professional Learning, and the related Innovation Configuration (available online at www.learningforward.org). These tools help educators develop a vision of the principal's role in creating highly effective schools and the strategies essential for them to learn. Once teams are grounded in the research, they can begin the five-stage systematic process of developing a theory of change.

The district team may want to identify a facilitator experienced in developing leadership skills to assist with the work. Since the intent of developing a theory of change is to clearly articulate the essential goals and interventions for achieving change, the facilitator may help ensure that each stage is accomplished thoughtfully and may ask questions that propel the group forward.

After drafting the theory, the team may consider distributing a copy throughout the district to ensure everyone's ideas are considered.

REFLECTIONS

Reflect on your assumptions about a principal's daily life and need for professional learning. Use your journal or the space below.

What assumptions are barriers for you?

What do you want to understand more deeply?

STRATEGIES AND INVESTIGATIONS

» Convene a focus group with principals in your area, and explore their perceptions about their work, their learning, and their needs. Ask the principals' view of coaching as a strategy for helping lead high-achieving schools.

- What do principals say about their daily lives?
- What are their needs, hopes, and/or learning aspirations?
- What trends do you see in your conversations with them?
- What systems would support your development of school principals?

» Follow an elementary school principal, a middle school principal, and a high school principal for a day.

- What observations can you make about principals' daily lives across all levels?
- What did you observe during conversations and during the principals' interactions with staff, students, parents, central office, and community leaders that would open the door for coaching conversations?

» Find out where there are districts that emphasize principal professional learning. Describe their theory of change and strategies for learning. Ask principals in that district about the effect of professional learning on their skills as a principal. Evaluate their theory of change for strengths and weaknesses.

» Explore the concept of theory of change on the Internet or in reading. Host conversations with principals about what professional learning experiences best meet their needs. Study how adults learn best and what strategies make the most sense for principal professional learning.

» Develop a theory of change about principal professional learning. Share it with principals, get their feedback, and make modifications in their work.

» Develop a plan of action for supporting principals in your district. What next steps are you ready to take to support principals, their learning, and their leadership? Do you want to start by learning more? Can you establish a district leadership team of central support and principals, and facilitate the group as members develop a theory of change for principal learning? If you have responsibility for principal learning, might you revise your own theory of change and integrate it into a district professional development plan?

STRATEGIES AND INVESTIGATIONS

» Consider what you might offer your district to allow the district to develop a plan of action for principal learning. Ideas might be to design a summer principals intensive academy, set up study teams among principals, or establish a coaching academy for future coaches of principals. To whom do you need to make these offers? What resources and support do you need?

TOOL
Template for developing a vision of principal professional learning and a theory of change

The purpose of professional learning for principals is:

_____

_____

_____

Based on our research on what matters in principal learning, our assumptions are:

_____

_____

_____

Our vision is:

_____

_____

_____

Principals would be ...

_____

_____

_____

Central support would ...

_____

_____

Our theory of change is:

_____

_____

_____

ActKnowledge. *Theory of change community.* Available online at www.theoryofchange.org.

Carter, G. (2009, February). *Is it good for the kids? The challenge of professional growth in a shrinking economy.* Alexandria, VA: ASCD.

Hall, P. (2004). *Always strive to be a better you.* Available online at www.educationworld.com/a_issues/chat/chat142.shtml.

Peterson, K.D. (2001, winter). The roar of complexity. *Journal of Staff Development, 22*(1), 18-21.

Rosa, M. (with Celio, M.B., Harvey, J., & Wishon, S.). (2003, January). *A matter of definition: Is there truly a shortage of school principals?* Seattle, WA: Center on Reinventing Public Education, Daniel J. Evans School of Public Affairs, University of Washington.

Sparks, D. (2007). *Leading for results: Transforming teaching, learning, and relationships in schools* (2nd ed.). Thousand Oaks, CA: Corwin Press & NSDC.

"Man cannot discover new oceans unless he has the courage
to lose sight of the shore."

— *Andre Gide, French critic, essayist, & novelist*

Jerome Jackson* was eager to learn more about the school where he
had just been hired to replace the principal, who was retiring after 25 years.
Jackson set aside a day to shadow the principal, hoping to glean valuable
lessons from her and get some insight into the school history. Jackson had a
list of questions ready. He asked her to tell him about the staff, the school's
goals, to describe the students and parents, and to talk about how she
managed her time and the day's routines. The retiring principal gave him
a tired look. "I start my day reading the newspaper in my office," she said.
"After about an hour, I go out on the playground and visit with the students.

The names in the examples throughout this book have been changed to allow anonymity.

Here are the two keys I use. This is my office. I make sure every day that every classroom has a teacher, and that is all I am concerned about."

Two years later, Jackson felt he still didn't know all he needed to know. Not understanding the dynamics of the parent group, he'd alienated some key stakeholders and was working to repair those relationships. He had taken on some reorganizing of support staff schedules that proved challenging, although the school was beginning to see the benefits. And he'd established a leadership committee that was implementing changes in teachers' professional learning that he was sure would pay dividends for students very soon. He still felt like each situation was full of hidden traps, however, and wished he had more of the background knowledge and skills to make decisions comfortably.

Today's principals are challenged to be courageous, visionary, and results-oriented leaders who make sure every child experiences high-quality teaching and learning every day. In an age of school reform, research has pointed specifically to the teacher as having the greatest influence on student achievement (Hord & Sommers, 2008; Marzano, Waters, & McNulty, 2005). Research on schools with high-performing teachers finds that the principal has the greatest influence on teachers' effectiveness (Leithwood, Louis, Anderson, & Wahlstrom, 2004). The quality of a principal affects a range of school outcomes, including teachers' satisfaction and their decisions about where to work, parents' perceptions about the schools their children attend, and, ultimately, the school's academic performance (Reeves, 2009).

Tim Waters, Robert Marzano, and Brian McNulty's research on school leaders (2003) found a strong correlation between skillful principals and student achievement. They identified 21 specific leadership responsibilities that significantly correlate with student achievement (see Table 3.1). Just as significantly, the authors also conclude that principals can have a marginal or even negative impact on student learning: "When school leaders concentrate on the wrong school or classroom practices or miscalculate the magnitude of the change required of those in the organization, achievement may be negatively impacted" (p. 7).

Principals' top priority in creating high-achieving schools is leading others to be learners (Institute for Educational Leadership, 2000). The Institute for Educational Leadership specifies three key roles that 21st-century principals should fulfill:

1. **Instructional leadership** that focuses on strengthening teaching and learning, professional development, data-driven decision making, and accountability;
2. **Community leadership** that focuses on awareness of the school's role in society; close relations with students, parents, community partners, and others; and advocacy for school capacity building and resources; and

TABLE 3.1 **Principal leadership responsibilities**

Responsibility	The extent to which the principal:
Culture	Fosters shared beliefs and a sense of community and cooperation.
Order	Establishes a set of standard operating procedures and routines.
Discipline	Protects teachers from issues and influences that would detract from their teaching time or focus.
Resources	Provides teachers with materials and professional development necessary to successfully execute their jobs.
Curriculum, instruction, and assessment	Is directly involved in the design and implementation of curriculum, instruction, and assessment practices.
Focus	Establishes clear goals and keeps those goals in the forefront of the school's attention.
Knowledge of curriculum, instruction, and assessment	Is knowledgeable about current curriculum, instruction, and assessment practices.
Visibility	Has quality contact and interactions with teachers and students.
Contingent reward	Recognizes and rewards individual accomplishments.
Communication	Establishes strong lines of communication with teachers and among students.
Outreach	Is an advocate and spokesperson for the school with all stakeholders.
Input	Involves teachers in the design and implementation of important decisions and policies.
Affirmation	Recognizes and celebrates school accomplishments and acknowledges failures.
Relationship	Demonstrates an awareness of the personal aspects of teachers and staff.
Change agents	Is willing to and actively challenges the status quo.
Optimizer	Inspires and leads new and challenging innovations.
Ideals/beliefs	Communicates and operates from strong ideals and beliefs about schooling.
Monitors/evaluates	Monitors the effectiveness of school practices and their impact on student learning.
Flexibility	Adapts his and her leadership behavior to the needs of the current situation and is comfortable with dissent.
Situational awareness	Is aware of the details and undercurrents in running the school and uses this information to address current and potential problems.
Intellectual stimulation	Ensures that faculty and staff are aware of the most current theories and practices, and makes the discussion of these a regular aspect of the school's culture.

Source: Waters, Marzano & McNulty, 2003. Adapted by permission of McREL.

Principals are expected to guide a coalition to
raise the performance of all students, and highly
effective leaders do.

3. **Visionary leadership** that exhibits passion and commitment, an entrepreneurial
   spirit, high energy, and a conviction that all children will learn at high levels.

Research from the National Association of Elementary Principals (2008) and
Waters, Marzano, and McNulty's research on effective principals (2003) also contribute to the knowledge base on school leadership, specifically principal effectiveness.
These studies clarify the skills, attitudes, and systems effective principals use to lead
high-achieving schools. All of the research reflects the challenges and complexities of
leading today's schools.

So what skills matter most?

Highly effective principals are systems thinkers, able to set goals, manage staff,
rally the community, create effective learning environments, and build support
systems for students. They are instructional leaders able to build learning coalitions
focused on student achievement and guide instruction so that students learn. They
lead teacher learning, engaging everyone in the school in purposeful collaboration
to achieve a compelling shared vision that leads to a culture of learning. They create
a culture that supports high student achievement. They are models of professional
growth, demonstrating what they want to see in others and sharing leadership
throughout the organization to strengthen all aspects of the school.

Here are attributes of highly effective principals.

SYSTEMS THINKERS

Principals are strong managers. They develop systems that establish solid routines
and operating procedures. While most principals say that focusing on student learning
and instruction is most important, a poorly managed school gets principals in trouble
and sometimes even fired. Designing and ensuring a schoolwide discipline management plan, developing a student schedule to ensure student success, efficiently using
staff, maintaining a school building and environment that highlights and celebrates
students, teachers, parents, and learning all are essential to a principal's success.

Adriana Lopez was a first-year principal, hired by a first-year
superintendent. Lopez' last job was as a secondary social studies teacher for
three years, and now she was responsible for leading a K-12 school of 700

students. Lopez and the superintendent were the only administrators in their district. Lopez spent two years understanding her new role, developing leadership skills, and working to ensure that the school was effectively managed. She then acknowledged the challenges that remained, most significantly skills that would lead to higher student achievement.

"When I figured out what the job really was and established routines and systems in the school for smooth operations," she said, "I then realized that developing curriculum and assessment design systems for teaching teams to continuously work on the work of teaching and learning would increase student learning significantly."

Engaging the assistance of a coach helped Lopez understand the importance of establishing systems for learning, as well as not lose sight of the essential skills she needed to develop to lead the entire faculty to a shared vision.

INSTRUCTIONAL LEADERS

Principals are expected to guide a coalition to raise the performance of all students, and highly effective leaders do. They monitor student performance continuously. They use student achievement data, inventories, and climate surveys to design school plans of action, plan staff learning experiences, create the schedules for students and staff to enable those experiences, budget the necessary resources, and extend learning time for students not meeting standards. They provide visible signs of the school's priority on student learning and success. Student work is visible throughout the school's hallways, signifying the importance of student learning. Student performance data on standardized tests are often visible in hallways and teacher work areas. Pictures of staff and student learning are featured throughout the school. They develop personal, caring, trusting relationships with all students in school and effectively communicate to all students the value of learning. These school leaders take personal responsibility for student achievement in the school and create a culture of high expectations for students, staff, parents, and community.

Alicia Copley was an assistant principal in a large high school. The high school students were very successful on standardized tests except in mathematics. Copley decided to work with the math teachers. The math teachers resisted her ideas. She was not an experienced mathematics teacher, and she did not know what she was talking about, they thought. Teachers were adamant that students were neither interested in nor willing to do what was expected in order to achieve higher scores on the state mathematics assessments. Copley sought a coach. She began to establish norms with the team that would lead them to learn together in positive ways. She asked them to look at the data with her to see if there were just one or two things that they could do differently together. She realized they did not have strong understandings of the standards tested or strong instructional strategies. She worked systematically with them to analyze the state content standards, determine what they look like when students are doing them well, and to address effective instruction. The team visited several teachers of mathematics whose students had high scores. They began to examine the instructional strategies they observed. The progress seemed very slow to Copley. The team would move forward and then balk. However, at the end of the year, student scores on the state standardized test dramatically improved. Though Copley still did not have a strong, trusting relationship with these staff members, she had their respect and was continuing their learning journey.

LEADERS OF TEACHER LEARNING

Effective principals understand and use Learning Forward's Standards for Professional Learning (www.learningforward.org/standards/standards.cfm) as a guide for designing learning experiences for themselves and others. They organize the staff in small learning teams as a primary strategy for professional learning. They use established norms and protocols to facilitate learning and problem solving. They embed lesson study, walk-throughs, critical friends groups, and analysis of student work as strategic processes for community learning. In addition, they monitor change in themselves and others and use the data to adjust personal plans and/or the school plan.

They ensure that teachers expand their deep knowledge of content as well as their skills in effective instructional strategies. They recognize that quality professional learning is key to supporting significant improvement in student performance.

Most importantly, leaders create a sense of urgency for change. They know the magnitude of the changes needed in the school and have a clear theory of change that will guide the change processes in the school. They challenge current thinking about the school's organization and the current strategies in light of the school's mission and vision, and keep the mission and vision at the forefront of conversations and in their actions. They ensure everyone in the school has a common sense of purpose, vision, and language in working with students and each other.

Matthew Barker was a courageous assistant principal. He was hired at the same time as the school principal, and the two joined forces to transform their low-performing high school. Barker soon realized, however, that most of the school's leadership team members had little experience facilitating professional learning or raising student achievement. Barker sought a coach to help him develop a clear plan of action to accelerate the learning of both students and staff. He felt he had only a little time to make

*Most importantly, leaders create a sense
of urgency for change.*

progress before the staff would begin to feel that they could not succeed.
The coach asked thoughtful questions about what Barker wanted people
to do, think, and learn together. Barker decided that he really wanted to
build a learning community that worked on the curriculum and assessment
strategies first. He felt that developing a learning community would give
him the greatest leverage. Together with his coach, he designed a plan of
action for himself. He began working with a small group of teachers whose
students' achievement on state assessments was the most dismal. He led the
team to focus on state standards, develop a curriculum map aligned with
the assessment calendar, and develop formative assessments for learning
to monitor student progress. When the teachers resisted his guidance, he
called on his coach to problem solve with him. He began to make headway.
At the end of the year, the team was surprised at how well students
performed on the state assessments. More teachers began seeking Barker's
assistance. Soon Barker was creating learning experiences for many teams in
the building, and student achievement increases were accelerating.

MODELS OF PROFESSIONAL GROWTH

Because skilled principals make learning central to all efforts in their school, they
place a high priority on personal learning as well as others' learning. They model
living by core values that promote achievement for every child, collaboration, and
persistence in reaching challenging goals. They establish personal goals, seek others'
assistance, and gather evidence of growth for reflection. Principals who model learning
for others invite fellow principals to their schools to conduct walk-throughs and have
conversations about their observations. They are continuously in study groups with
other principals. They read and stay current in their field. They model personal growth
so that teachers in their schools see their principal learning.

Pam Moore was a model learner. She regularly shared information from
her latest reading with colleagues and asked them to join in discussions
of the material. She often explained to her staff that she and her learning
team were working to understand some concept of leadership and wanted
their ideas. Principals from other schools routinely observed her working
with a grade level or team of teachers and made notes so that Moore could
get an observer's feedback. When her teachers learned new skills, she was

right there with them in their learning. She volunteered to try the new strategy first and let teachers observe her. When she attended conferences, she was strategic in the sessions she attended so that they mattered in her leadership. Moore called herself the "head learner."

ABLE TO ESTABLISH LEARNING CULTURES

Powerful principals know the importance of school culture in ensuring student and staff success. They focus on building trust through effectively making and managing commitments, as well as coordinating action. They establish norms in the

ASSUMPTIONS

Effective principals:

» Focus intensely on student learning and build meaningful relationships with all students;

» Hold and build among all staff, students, and parents a compelling vision of the school as a community of learners with high expectations for all students;

» Place learning at the center of all change efforts;

» Ensure purposeful collaboration that engages everyone in the school — parents and community members who have a responsibility and an interest in school success, and of course, the students;

» Are systems thinkers;

» Are instructional leaders;

» Lead teacher learning;

» Model professional learning;

» Build a culture of learning; and

» Build leadership throughout the organization.

organization that promote a sense of community, confidence, competence, sincerity, and lightness. They eagerly engage students, parents, staff, and community as equal partners in achieving the mission and goals of the school. They model high levels of competence in facilitating the development of school-based curriculum, assessments of student learning, and research-based instruction that meets the needs of all students. They recognize and celebrate others' contributions to achieving the school goals. They use meaningful ceremonies and storytelling as a strategy for celebration. They foster enthusiasm for learning in all in the school. Most importantly, they stay the course long enough for new strategies or innovations to become the new culture by developing a vision in others of the change process, clarifying expectations, and supporting others by modeling and coaching.

Miranda Garza knew the importance of a strong relationship with the teachers in her building. She planned opportunities for staff to share stories and successes by encouraging teaching teams to share what they were doing at parent nights or to take the lead during staff meetings. She also knew the significance of a clearly articulated and aligned curriculum for the school's students, many of whom were challenged to succeed academically. Garza worked with the faculty over seven years to develop and refine a system that includes common units of study, common assessments *of* and *for* learning, and common lesson plans so that teams can examine gaps in student learning. The federal government recognized the school for exemplary leadership in increasing the achievement of English language learners.

ABLE TO SHARE LEADERSHIP

Powerful principals value leadership in others. They know that as others develop leadership skills and take leadership roles, the school becomes stronger. They intentionally facilitate leadership emerging from all aspects of the organization. They encourage and facilitate teacher leadership and help those seeking to become principals develop skills. They self-reflect, assess their successes and failures, and use their assessments to learn and set goals for themselves. They listen to develop deeper understanding of themselves and others. They continuously seek to expand personal observations and viewpoints of life with an open mind toward possibilities. They use humor and laughter to facilitate a joyful journey, a grateful journey, and to lighten the loads of those around them.

Ty Embry had been principal for several years in a school where student achievement was improving on standardized tests. However, Embry was concerned that he could not lead teachers to make changes that would continue to raise achievement and help all students. He found a coach. His coach began to explore with Embry strategies for staff learning that Embry would like to see in the school. He was unclear about the request, so the coach asked the principal to research effective professional learning before they began designing a plan.

Embry began eagerly. Soon, he called the coach to request time with her. Through her questioning, he began to determine a vision of what he wanted staff to do that he believed would make a difference in their learning and energize them. Because the staff had little experience with effective professional learning, Embry wanted to start work with the leadership team and start small.

The coach guided him through designing a plan. Embry decided to use regular walk-throughs and record data about teachers' instructional strategies. He asked his school leadership team to participate. After several months of gathering data, Embry and the leadership team presented their findings to the staff and designed an inquiry process to help lead staff to new learning strategies. The staff was intrigued by the data and began to work in small teams to research more effective instructional strategies for teaching reading and writing.

Because Embry developed leadership skills, the staff slowly began to select strategies that were meaningful to them. They began to observe one another teaching, to design lessons together, and to coach one another to implement the strategies with fidelity. All the teachers became more proficient in their use of the new strategies. Everyone was engaged and energized. Everyone was learning. Everyone felt committed to his or her own learning, confident that the teaching strategies could make a significant difference in student learning.

The coach began reflection strategies with Embry, asking: What about your leadership made the difference? What would you do again? What would you do differently? What are you learning? What are you ready to learn now?

When school leaders concentrate on developing their competence in system thinking, instructional leadership, leading professional learning, sharing leadership, developing culture, and modeling learning, they have a significant impact on teacher learning and effectiveness, which in turn leads to improved student learning. These responsibilities of highly effective principals highlight the challenges principals face in being able to do the job in the absence of collaboration, support, and coaching (Sparks, 2002).

REFLECTIONS

In what ways am I a model learner for others? How do I inspire others to learn through my own actions?

How do I share and build leadership in others?

In what ways do I listen to principals to know where the systems in their schools are not supporting student and staff learning?

In your journal, reflect on your own strengths from your time as a school administrator. What were your challenges? Your weaknesses? What kinds of conversations, coaching experiences, and/or support would have been most helpful? Generate your own examples and stories, and record them for future use.

STRATEGIES AND INVESTIGATIONS

» Establish your own assumptions about school leadership. Ground these assumptions in readings and research.

» Review what you are learning with your coaching community. Engage them in a discussion of what highly effective principals do to lead powerful learning communities. Share your research and findings from your readings and from your shadowing experiences.

» Consider what you each hold in common. Design a vision of support strategies that would strengthen your understanding of leadership and the challenges principals face.

» Shadow another principal within your coaching community. Debrief the experience with the principal. Reflect on what you are learning.

» Make notes in your journal about what you are learning, what you wish to learn more about, and what next steps you might take.

» Review your goal to see if you want to revise it or to review your progress on achieving it.

» Investigate the research on the skills of effective leaders. Start with research listed in the resources section of this chapter. What about this research validates your thinking, learning, and experiences? What surprises you? Discuss your responses with your study team. Make notes in your journal of areas to explore more deeply.

» Shadow two or three highly effective principals. You might select principals at different levels, from different size schools, or from different areas, such as urban and suburban schools. Make notes about their skills, attitudes, and dispositions. Note how they focus on student learning, how they build and maintain shared vision, how they instill professional learning into the school's daily life, how they engage others in powerful collaboration, what types of celebrations are important to them, how they encourage leadership in others, how they focus strategic efforts, and how they balance management with a focus on student learning. Interview these principals about their perceptions of school leadership and their views of their strengths and challenges. Ask them what support they have or would like

STRATEGIES AND INVESTIGATIONS

to have to be more effective. Discuss your findings with your study group. Record what you learn in your journal.

» Create a graphic organizer reflecting the essential skills, attitudes, and dispositions of highly effective principals. Review and revise it regularly. Note references and research for later exploration and deeper study.

» Establish a section in your journal to capture strategic, focused coaching questions. You may want to organize questions around certain topics: Questions that expect the coachee to listen more closely to others, questions that would guide a coachee to see a different point of view, etc.

TOOL A principal's self-assessment and plan of action template

Use this template to help self-assess where you are and to shape your vision of what you would do to lead a high-performing school. Make notes in the appropriate box for each category. Be specific and give examples. You do not need to make notes for every descriptor.

	EXEMPLARY	PROFICIENT	EMERGING	UNSATISFACTORY
	Exceeds expectations Unique, creative, inventive. Always or consistently exhibits…	**Meets standard expectations.** Generally, often, usually models or exhibits…	**Below expectations.** Sometimes frequently, occasionally, or inconsistently exhibits…	**A concern.** Infrequently, inconsistently, unintentionally, accidentally, unpredictably, or rarely exhibits…
A collective focus on student learning.				
• Monitors student performance continuously.				
• Uses student achievement data, inventories, and climate surveys to design school plans of action, staff learning experiences, and schedules for students and staff; budgets resources; and allows extended learning time for students who are not successful.				
• Visibly places a high priority on student learning and success in school.				
• Develops personal, caring, trusting relationships with all students in the school.				
• Effectively communicates to all students the true value of learning.				
• Takes personal responsibility for student achievement in the school.				
• Creates a culture of high expectations for students, staff, parents, and the community.				

	EXEMPLARY	PROFICIENT	EMERGING	UNSATISFACTORY
A shared mission, goals, vision, values.				
• Creates and facilitates a professional learning community to ensure everyone in the school has a common sense of purpose, vision, and language in working with students and each other.				
• Models living by the core values of the school community.				
• Creates a sense of urgency for change.				
• Facilitates the development of effective change strategies.				
• Keeps visible the vision and mission through conversations and printed materials about the school.				
• Seeks opportunities to highlight progress toward achieving the school's goals.				

	EXEMPLARY	PROFICIENT	EMERGING	UNSATISFACTORY
A shared focus on professional learning.				
• Places a high priority on personal learning, as well as learning in others.				
• Ensures that teachers expand their knowledge of their content, as well as their skill in using effective instructional strategies.				
• Insists that and facilitates regular monitoring of gains in student learning.				
• Recognizes quality professional learning is key to supporting significant improvement in student performance.				
• Establishes personal goals, seeks assistance from others, and gathers evidence of growth for reflection.				
• Models personal growth and construction of innovative practices to learn.				
• Participates in and leads others in book studies.				
• Organizes time (Learning Forward's standard for time for professional learning is 25% of the day) and manages the energy in the organization to engage staff in powerful conversations and professional learning.				
• Uses Learning Forward's Standards for Professional Learning as guides for designing learning experiences for themselves and others.				
• Organizes the staff in small learning teams as a primary strategy for staff development.				
• Embeds lesson study, walk-throughs, critical friends groups, action research, tuning protocols, and analysis of student work as strategic processes for communities to learn.				
• Monitors change in self and others, and uses the data to adjust personal plans and/or the school plan.				

	EXEMPLARY	PROFICIENT	EMERGING	UNSATISFACTORY
A culture of collaboration, persistence, and celebration.				
• Builds trust through effectively making and managing commitments, as well as coordinating action.				
• Establishes norms in the organization that promote a sense of community, confidence, competence, and sincerity.				
• Eagerly engages students, parents, staff, and community as equal partners in achieving the school's mission and goals.				
• Models high levels of competence in developing school-based curricula, assessments of student learning, and research-based instruction that meets the needs of all students.				
• Recognizes and celebrates others' contributions to achieving school goals.				
• Fosters enthusiasm for learning throughout the school.				
• Stays the course long enough for new strategies or innovations to become part of the culture.				
• Develops a vision in others of the change process, clarifies expectations, and supports others through modeling and coaching.				
• Establishes ceremonies and storytelling as a strategy for celebration.				

	EXEMPLARY	PROFICIENT	EMERGING	UNSATISFACTORY
A culture of collective inquiry and strategic school planning.				
• Uses inquiry and constructivist strategies to research best practices and explore areas of greatest need and interest in the school.				
• Facilitates the school community to be skillful consumers of education research.				
• Ensures that the school plan aligns with the district's mission, goals, and strategies.				
• Uses data and grounded educational research to make decisions about the direction of the school plan and the needs of students, staff, and parents.				
• Disaggregates data to ensure equitable treatment of all groups of students and to extend learning opportunities to students before they fall too far behind in their learning.				
• Engages all stakeholders in school inquiry and planning.				
• Facilitates focusing the school plan on student needs.				
• Reallocates school resources to ensure the school's goals are achieved.				
• Regularly and consistently monitors progress and uses problem-solving strategies to discover and overcome barriers to achieving the mission.				

	EXEMPLARY	PROFICIENT	EMERGING	UNSATISFACTORY
A disposition toward transformational leadership and reflective dialogue.				
• Encourages and facilitates leadership emerging from all aspects of the organization.				
• Engages staff, students, parents, and the community in conversations about the school's progress toward achieving the mission.				
• Values courage and risk taking to ensure that the organization is moving toward its mission.				
• Facilitates the development of skills, attitudes, and dispositions in others to lead professional development and mentor peers.				
• Facilitates transitions in leader positions such as department and PTA leaders to ensure continuous focus and direction.				
• Encourages and facilitates the development of others seeking leadership positions, especially the principalship.				
• Shares and reflects with other principals to facilitate the exponential learning of all.				
• Humbly self-reflects and honestly assesses successes and failures, and uses both to reflect on personal learning.				
• Carefully listens to others to develop a deeper understanding of self and others.				
• Continuously seeks to expand personal observations and viewpoints of life with an open mind.				
• Uses humor and laughter to facilitate a joyful, grateful journey and to lighten the loads of self and others.				

Visioning organizer and critical attributes chart for highly effective principals

My vision of the role of a highly effective principal:

Skills	Dispositions	Attitudes and aspirations

The support that would have helped me the most is:

_____

_____

Why?

_____

_____

The support that others value is:

_____

_____

Why?

_____

_____

My additional reflections about my strengths as a coach:

_____

_____

My vision of my role as a coach:

My skills	My dispositions	My attitudes and aspirations

My strengths:

_____

_____

_____

My weaknesses:

_____

_____

_____

My summary

Overall strengths	Challenges

My professional learning plan

1. The area(s) I want to focus on this year are:

   _____

   _____

   _____

2. My goals are:

   _____

   _____

   _____

3. My vision is: (What will I be doing, thinking, etc. when I am achieving my goal?)

   _____

   _____

   _____

4. My plan of action:

   _____

   _____

   _____

Theory of change

Learning strategies reflect a thoughtful, grounded theory of change. The strategies answer the questions:

- How will we get from where we are to where we want to be?
- What will it take for me and my leadership team to authentically incorporate our new learning into our everyday work?

Expected impact on my leadership, teacher practice, and student learning:

_____

_____

_____

Logic model

Principals set a logical pathway or model for accomplishing their goals by breaking their theory of change into checkpoints.

10 months from now	7 months from now	3 months from now	Essential resources	Inputs
Long-term outcomes (student achievement gains expected and shifts in teacher practices)	_Intermediate goals_	_Short-term goals_		
Measures of effectiveness				
Artifacts				

Benefits	Impediments to accomplishing my goal(s)	Essential involvement I need from others
To students		
To me		
To the school team		

Checkpoints for ascertaining progress	Evidence I will accept that I am achieving my goal(s)	Thoughts about my portfolio

RESOURCES FOR CHAPTER 3

Chirichello, M. (2004, Spring). Collective leadership: Reinventing the principalship. *Kappa Delta Pi Record, 40*(3), 119-123.

Copeland, M. (2001). The myth of the superprincipal. *Phi Delta Kappan, 82*(7), 528-533.

Drath, W.H. (2001). *The deep blue sea: Rethinking the source of leadership.* San Francisco: Jossey-Bass.

Ferrandino, V. (2003). The embattled principal. *Principal, 83*(1), 70.

Lambert, L. (2003). *Leadership capacity for lasting school improvement.* Alexandria, VA: ASCD.

SECTION 2
Attributes of successful coaches

"Those who can most truly be accounted brave are those who best know the meaning of what is sweet in life and what is terrible, and then go out, undeterred, to meet what is to come."

— *Pericles*

"Listening can be a way of life, an attitude toward all things, an open posture to the world. We can listen fully to the joy and pain of other people, to our thoughts and emotions, to our bodies, to nature, to music, to circumstances, to the lessons of the past, to our dreams of the future."

— *Ellis, 2000*

Xavier Brooks, a veteran high school principal, was closing in on the end of a great school year. The school had won several honors, including becoming a national Blue Ribbon School. The dropout rate was down, college acceptance rates were up, and Brooks was excited about the future. Then, just a few days before graduation, a senior with an outstanding record and a scholarship to a prestigious university brought a pellet gun to school and shot at the tires of a loading school bus.

Brooks immediately led a disciplinary hearing. School and district policies required that the student be suspended. If he were suspended, he would be unable to complete his finals, unable to graduate, and would likely lose his scholarship. The team of teachers in the hearing, wanting the best for this student, decided to give him detention.

Word spread quickly within the small, tight-knit community, and soon phones were ringing in both the principal's and superintendent's office about the incident. Parents wanted to know why policy had not been followed, when other exceptions had been made, and how the school determined which students were allowed to get by with breaking the rules. The superintendent, who had not been privy to the process, backed Brooks and assured callers that he was confident Brooks had followed policy. Brooks also found that the high school staff was divided.

Realizing the urgency of the quickly escalating situation, Brooks called in his coach to help him untangle the difficulties. Brooks and his coach began to identify all the issues, the breakdowns in communication and processes, and to establish a vision of a win-win situation for everyone, including the student. With the coach's strategic questioning, Brooks began to structure new actions. He recognized that trust with different stakeholder groups had been violated in many ways, and rebuilding that would not be easy. He immediately drafted a statement that he had violated policy and stated the reason as an effort to act in the student's best interest. He prepared data on the history of behavior issues at the school and related disciplinary actions to be shared publicly to reassure the community about past actions. He set up a meeting with his superintendent to prepare a statement for the school board, and Brooks and the superintendent together called a news conference. In the end, Brooks and the superintendent decided that the student was not permitted to participate in graduation, but the youth did complete his finals and retain his scholarship.

Skillful coaching helps those from novice to veteran. Coaching can support leaders in the snarl of crises and those working on long-term change. Becoming such a skillful coach requires that coaches develop their own emotional intelligence and develop their abilities to observe, listen, question, and help leaders envision a different outcome.

Developing these skills is challenging. A desire to help others solve their problems can get in the way of coaching; it seems faster just to tell personal stories or relate experiences and solve the problem. Even everyday conversations often reflect this approach: "Well, if I were you…" "When I was in your shoes, I…" "One way I solved that problem was to…" "Haven't you tried to…" "You really ought to…" Although these offers are often appreciated, they are not useful coaching strategies as they are grounded in assumptions that someone other than the individual can solve one's own problems and that one person's experiences are applicable to another's.

A desire to help others solve their
problems can get in the way of coaching.

Develop emotional intelligence

Effective coaches understand and develop emotional intelligence. People with high levels of emotional intelligence are *self-aware, self-regulated, self-motivated,* have *social awareness,* and have *highly developed social skills* (Goleman, 1995).

Self-awareness. Self-awareness involves recognizing emotions and how feelings are linked to what we think, do, and say. Emotions affect performance. Effective coaches reflect and learn from their experience, and they are open to candid feedback and new perspectives. Although they are serious about their purpose and make meaningful commitments in their lives, they exhibit a sense of humor and live in lightness. Others view them as self-assured. They are not afraid to voice unpopular views, go out on a limb for what is right, and make sound decisions despite uncertainties and pressures. At the same time, they do not see themselves as others' "saviors," but as skilled guides to help others develop greater self-awareness and become competent in making effective decisions. Self-awareness is both a trait of a skilled coach and a skill a coach wishes to develop in leaders. When coaches attend to their own moods, language, and health, they model what want to see in those they coach. When they check themselves for optimism, hopefulness, and enthusiasm and then self-adjust, they are in the best position to be totally present with those they coach.

Self-regulation. Coaches who effectively self-regulate manage impulsive feelings and distressing emotions; they remain composed and positive even in trying moments. While they consistently act ethically and are above reproach, they admit their mistakes. They build trust by acting reliable and authentic — they meet commitments and keep promises, hold themselves accountable for meeting their objectives, and are flexible in how they see events. They smoothly handle multiple demands, shifting priorities, and rapid change.

Self-motivation. Effective coaches are self-motivated. They are results-oriented, set challenging goals, take calculated risks, and explore original solutions. They pursue information to reduce uncertainty, learn ways to improve their performance, and readily make personal sacrifices. Although they are self-motivated and goal-oriented, they see themselves as members of a larger community, such as a school, church, or city, and they know that they are only one of many working to meet a larger organizational goal. They find a sense of purpose in the larger mission, use the *group's* core values to make decisions and clarify choices, pursue goals beyond what is required or expected of them, and mobilize others. They persist in seeking goals despite obstacles and setbacks, and they operate based on the hope of success rather than fear of failure.

Social awareness. Social awareness is an essential aspect of emotional intelligence. Individuals who are socially aware sense others' feelings and perspectives and take an active interest in others' concerns. Coaches who are socially aware listen well, are attentive to leaders' emotional cues, understand others' perspectives, and demonstrate sensitivity. They acknowledge and reward people's strengths and accomplishments, offer useful feedback, identify people's needs for development, create an environment of respect where diverse people can thrive, and accurately read key power relationships.

Social skills. Coaches with high levels of emotional intelligence also are socially skillful. They use effective persuasion strategies, use simple processes and strategies to build consensus and support, and effectively make their point. They send clear and convincing messages, deal with difficult issues straightforwardly, listen well, seek mutual understanding, welcome full sharing of information, foster open communication, and stay receptive to bad news as well as good (Goleman, 1995).

Observe

David Rock, chief executive officer of Results Coaching Systems and author of *Quiet Leadership* (HarperCollins, 2006), researched the impact of experiences on decision making and concludes that we see the world as *we* are, not as the world is. Julio Olalla, founder of Newfield Ontological Coaching, states that our observations are shaped by our own experiences, values, and culture (2003a).

These authors and coaches find that when data enters the brain, we compare the new information to existing maps or observations of the world and seek to connect the new information with the existing frameworks. This efficiency enables the brain to manage thousands of pieces of data continuously, but leads to challenges as well. We resist change because of our hardwired ways of thinking. Although external conditions change, people's internal realities often do not. When we experience big shifts and changes in our world, we need time to rewire our minds, to make new connections.

Finally, given that brain wiring is different from person to person, any group of people may see the exact same situation in the world with substantially different perspectives (Rock, 2006).

"The brain truly seeks the world according to its own wiring," Rock states (p. 18). "In fact, the majority of the time, it's even worse than that — our brains will go to great pains to vehemently defend our existing mental models even to the point, at times, of death."

While it is impossible to change hard wiring, according to Rock the challenge is to build new maps. Since the brain is continuously creating new connections, the best way to develop new habits is not by trying to rid the mind of old maps, but by building new ones.

William Glasser's concepts of reality therapy and choice theory (1998) give coaches a construct to become different observers of the world, and to help leaders do so. Reality therapy enumerates five basic needs people share:

- **Power:** Achievement and feeling worthwhile;
- **Belonging:** From groups, families, and loved ones;
- **Freedom:** Independence, autonomy;
- **Fun:** Pleasure and enjoyment; and
- **Survival:** Nourishment, shelter, sex.

We all continually act to meet these basic needs. Because we are unaware so much of the time of why we act the way we do, we do not always make the best choices. For example, a child acting out in class may be doing so because he or she is not achieving in school and feels powerless. Sitting alone in the evening and "depressing," as Glasser would say, is not a good way to make new friends and meet the need for love and belonging, yet many choose these behaviors without recognizing that they are not meeting their need.

The skillful coach becomes an observer of his or her own behavior, learns to recognize unmet needs, and then can help those being coached see *their* behaviors, needs, and different options. Doing so helps both coach and the leader develop more successful strategies.

Listen

Extraordinary coaching depends on coaches' ability to listen between the lines to clarify the speaker's intended meaning and to discern the leader's observations of his or her world. Effective listeners listen with all their senses. They listen for what is not being said; they listen for assessments — or judgments — others are making of the world. Our basic needs shape the way we assess situations and either open or close opportunities based on our viewpoint. The effective coach helps bring to light the assessments underlying decisions. The coach determines how the speaker is grounding his or her assessments and how the speaker is justifying and explaining his or her thinking and emotions. For example:

Leader: We have tried and tried to get our superintendent to allow us to have time on the agenda just to share ideas. He never lets us.

Coach: How many times have you asked?

The effective coach uses data to help ground an assessment. For example:

Leader: The parents of those children just do not care about …

Coach: What data do you have that would support that statement?

Highly effective coaches make an intentional decision to be totally present with the client and to listen to all that is to be heard. How do coaches stay fully present?

Pause and reflect

What does it feel like when you are fully present in the moment?

When have you felt fully present?

What was that experience like?

What do you learn about yourself on such occasions?

What do you learn about others in such situations?

What keeps you from being fully present?

How can you overcome those barriers?

They give the other person all the "air space." They do not bring concerns from their own life into the coaching situation or offer solutions that have worked for *them*. They avoid making judgments or asking questions too quickly. They block out their own challenges and shut off their inner voice. These types of listeners learn exquisitely. Their world is big and full of things to hear.

Many times coaches feel they have the answer to a situation, even cutting off the leader's thoughts or interrupting an explanation to offer a solution. When the coach makes an intentional decision to be present and listen without feeling the need to teach, facilitate, interfere, or interpret, the coach learns about the leader's thinking and problem-solving strategies. The leader's confidence grows. The coach and leader get to know one another in a different way. Asking for greater clarification or more information opens the door to enthusiastic conversation and the joy of shared thinking. What experiences have you had with being fully present? Stop and reflect for a few minutes. Use the questions for reflection in the box at left.

Question

Skillful questioning is a central skill in coaching. New coaches often are concerned about becoming expert questioners. Instead of genuinely listening to the conversation, they spend their time thinking about what questions they should ask. Questioning is an essential component of effective coaching, but thoughtful questions emerge naturally from careful listening.

Effective coaches know that the expert best able to solve the problem is the individual being coached. Coaches who ask questions instead of providing answers honor those being coached and let them know they are able to solve their own issues and become the leaders and people they wish to be. Tony Stoltzfus (2008) says he has found that most people are able to solve their problems, but they need support and courage to change.

"But roughly 80% of the time, I find that they already know what to do," Stoltzfus says. "They just don't have the confidence to step out and do it. Self-confidence is a huge factor in change. When you ask for people's opinions and take them seriously, you are sending a powerful message: 'You have great ideas. I believe in you. You can do it.' Just asking can empower people to do things they couldn't do on their own" (2008, p. 9).

Effective questions come from the coach's natural curiosity about the leader's concerns, dreams, and aspirations. The coach's questions may be aimed at getting to know the leader, his or her values, life goals, and future plans. Questioning also may help the leader begin to focus more deeply on those areas.

Some early questions might be:

- What do you really want for your life?
- What does it look like to you?
- What would you be doing? Thinking?
- What is holding you back?
- What values hold you constant?
- What keeps you vigilant about your thinking, actions, and attitudes?
- What are your dreams and aspirations for your life?
- What are your passions about being a principal?
- What do you want most for your school?
- What do you love about your school?
- What are your school's greatest assets?

ASSUMPTIONS

- » Emotional intelligence and skills in observing, listening, questioning, and envisioning can be learned — and coaches who want to be powerful coaches will seek to learn new skills.

- » Coaches' personal growth will enable them to more effectively help others.

- » Leaders both want and are able to effectively solve their own problems.

- » Leaders need the skills and confidence to solve their own problems.

- » Powerful questions emerge out of powerful listening.

- » Grounded assessments help people see situations in new ways.

- What are your school's greatest challenges?
- How do you best face challenges in your life?
  The coach may want to explore some significant areas by asking:
- What are the most significant events in your life?
- What makes them so for you?
- What is the best thing about you? Your family?
- Who are your role models?
- Who has shaped your life?
- What about those people matters to you?

Another conversation may help the coach discover the leader's hopes for the coaching session. The coach may ask:

- What is important to you about our time together?
- What outcomes do you hope for from our work together?

Envision

Skilled coaches help others envision options for their world. Many books on leadership highlight the power of vision and shared vision; however, many school leaders have difficulty challenging themselves to envision schools that achieve new and different outcomes. A good coach reminds leaders of the power of one.

Muhammad Yunus, a Bangladeshi economist, had a vision of leading the people of his country out of poverty. The 2006 winner of the Nobel Peace Prize developed the concepts of microcredit and microfinance — of banks that would make small loans of up to a few hundred dollars to the poor without collateral to help them establish their own businesses. Yunus envisioned women leading the way with myriad small businesses that would help them lift their families out of poverty. He envisioned a different option to address a world issue that has plagued nations perpetually without any effective solutions having been found.

Like Yunus, skillful coaches are optimists who see creative solutions. Coaches envision new approaches to their own issues and varied strategies for achieving their own goals. They do not see many limitations to possibility. A highly skilled coach rarely says, "That just can't be done," "They won't let us do that," or "That is just not possible."

Visionary coaches watch for possibilities to emerge. Faced with difficult situations, they persevere. They recognize problems in solutions the leader suggests and, through inquiry, lead those they coach to search for new ideas, innovative strategies, and different pathways. Though a new solution may be a frightening experience, powerful coaches inspire others to be intrigued and motivated by possibilities.

REFLECTIONS

What big ideas am I taking away from these strategies?

What new skills am I eager to make my own?

What impact do I think these skills will have on my success in my own life?

What impact will these skills have on my effectiveness for coaching principals to ensure their success?

Consider the descriptors of emotional intelligence.

In your journal, reflect on these questions: Which areas are your strengths? Which areas would you like to strengthen? What actions might you take? When? With whom? What resources would you need? Reflect on what you are learning about yourself.

One of an effective coach's most powerful skills is observation. Reflect in your journal on how acute and precise an observer you believe you are.

STRATEGIES AND INVESTIGATIONS

» Establish a question section in your journal organized around Glasser's needs: power, belonging, freedom, fun. Use the questions in the table below and add others as you generate them. Listen to others' questions and record those that catch your attention.

Power	Belonging
What one thing could you do to move yourself closer to achieving your goal?	What strategies or steps would help you develop more meaningful relationships?
What have you always wanted to learn to do that you have not?	
What goals have you achieved that you felt good about? What attitude got you there? What skills did you learn? How did you persist?	
Freedom	**Fun**
What choices do you have in this situation that intrigue you?	What do you really enjoy doing?
	What does it feel like when you are doing what you enjoy?
What strategies might you use to expand your options?	
	What inspires you?
Which do you want to use?	
	What gives you energy?
Under what conditions could you do that?	

STRATEGIES AND INVESTIGATIONS

» Create a needs chart in your journal:

Power	Belonging
Freedom	Fun

- Observe how others satisfy these basic needs. How do they feed their need for power? For love and belonging? For freedom and fun? Where are their breakdowns in relationships with others?

- Next, chart your own needs. What drives you? How do you satisfy each of these needs? How do your assessments of your own issues close opportunities for you? What might happen if you made other assessments?

» Create organizers for your own questions. List questions under topic headers such as: Getting to know the person I am coaching, getting to know his or her concerns, questions that uncover successes, and challenges of the client.

» Create a photo album of significant people in your own life. Leave room on the pages for reflections. What about them has shaped your life? Your thinking? Your aspirations? What pictures bring stressful memories? How have you overcome those feelings? How have you reshaped images or visions from your past in ways that opened new opportunities for you?

STRATEGIES AND INVESTIGATIONS

» Use an organizer to envision your future.

I am a delightful, optimistic person who:

The vision I have for my life...			
In relationships with others is:	**In relationship to my work is:**	**As a learner is:**	**(Your choice)**
		As a coach is:	

» Write a brief autobiography. What experiences in your life shaped your viewpoint? How does your culture affect the choices you have made and are making?

» At least three or four times a week, look in a mirror. Make notes about your feet, your hands, your shoulders, and the way you hold your head. What do you observe about your emotions in your body? What shifts do you observe over time? What led to those shifts? What basic needs are you striving to meet? How does this striving show up in your mental, emotional, and physical condition?

» Challenge yourself to see an issue differently. Select a book you would not normally read. After reading it, consider what new observations you have about the world. What perceptions surprised you? Note any shifts in your optimism, your energy, your language. How have these shifts created a potential for new actions?

STRATEGIES AND INVESTIGATIONS

» Go to the mall, the airport, children's playground, the park or any public place where you can observe for a significant amount of time. Listen carefully. Make notes of what you hear. Note when you begin to judge, assess, or interpret, then refocus on being fully present and listening. What do you notice about your attention? What can you hear that you have never heard before? What can you see that you have never seen before?

» Challenge yourself emotionally and intellectually to use all of your senses several times every day by intensely, actively listening to others around you. Note when your attention wanders. What observations can you make about your listening skills? What new things do you hear?

» Have a conversation with a friend or your significant other without judging or assessing, and reflect on what you learn.

» Think about something in your life that you always wanted to do. What barriers prevented you from achieving your goal? Now envision achieving your goal. What would it take for you to make it happen right now? Under what conditions would you achieve your dream? Is the dream a worthy one? Would it benefit others? If it is worthwhile for you and others, do it! What new energy, dreams, and aspirations do you have?

» Ken Blanchard shares a strategy called "green light thinking" in his book, *Know Can Do!* He says that when we have an idea, a green light thinker says, "How can that work for us?" (Blanchard, Meyer, & Ruhe, 2007). Think of situations in which you have said, "That just can't happen," "They won't let us," or "I can't do that!" Apply green light thinking to those situations. What would it look like if you could? If you did? If they let you? What evidence do you have that they will not? What are your options?

» Judiciously listen to your own assessments of the world. When do you find yourself shutting down possibilities? When do you find you use positive mindsets? How does a positive mindset open opportunities for you? What new questions are you discovering because of these observations?

» What assessments have you made that limited your opportunities? What assessments have opened opportunities for you? Elaborate in your journal. Where do these assessments come from? Are they grounded?

» Record the implications of all your thinking in your coaching journal.

» Spend at least 30 minutes a day meditating. When you feel distracted, take note of what causes the distraction and then move yourself back to meditation.

STRATEGIES AND INVESTIGATIONS

» Some Native American cultures use a talking stick to signal who may speak. Find a partner or a small group and use the talking stick. The person holding the stick has the floor to speak as long as he or she wishes. Everyone else just listens. Once the person says all he or she wishes to say, that person passes the stick to someone else who has the same privilege. After everyone speaks, reflect with the group about the experience. What did it mean to each person to be fully heard? What did it mean to listen without interpreting or interrupting others?

» Select a place where you can anonymously observe others — a library, a social event, a park, the grocery store. Observe others' interactions as though you were watching a movie. Make notes in your journal about their body language, facial expressions, their posture, hand positions, gestures, and walk. What do their bodies tell you about them? What emotions do they create in you? How does their emotional intelligence show up in their bodies? Emotions? Word choice? How do they use language to relate to others? Look for coherence. What questions might you ask them to effectively coach them? Summarize what you learn.

» Watch a movie and observe the main character or a character that intrigues you. Record your observations. Concentrate on the character's choices. What needs drove that character to see those options? What options were not open to that character because of his or her assessments of the world?

» Ask a principal or someone in your study team to allow you to coach him or her. Work to sharpen your observation skills and to develop competence in asking questions that focus the coached person on how that person is meeting his or her basic needs. Use Glasser's needs chart to identify comments the individual makes that reflect breakdowns or barriers to achieving goals.

» Listen to conversations around you for assessments, and think of how those assessments create or prevent opportunities for those talking. Make notes in your journal of what questions you might ask that would shift their thinking.

» Pay attention to your own conversations for when you make ungrounded assessments. Begin to question others to help them ground their assessments. Note the impact of your questions on your own and others' thinking.

» Practice being present in your conversations. Notice the impact as your skill in listening grows. Notice shifts in your own attitudes toward others. Reflect on these experiences in your journal. Share what you learn with others in your peer coaching group.

RESOURCES FOR CHAPTER 4

Crane, T.G. (2010). *The heart of coaching: Using transformational coaching to create a high-performance coaching culture* (3rd ed.). San Diego, CA: FTA Press.

Ellis, D. (2000). *Falling awake.* Rapid City, SD: Breakthrough Enterprises.

Hart, L. (1978). *Human brain and human learning.* New York/London: Longman.

Pert, C.B. (1997). *Molecules of emotion.* New York: Scribner.

Pert, C.B. (2009). *Welcome to Candace Pert.* Available online at www.candacepert.com.

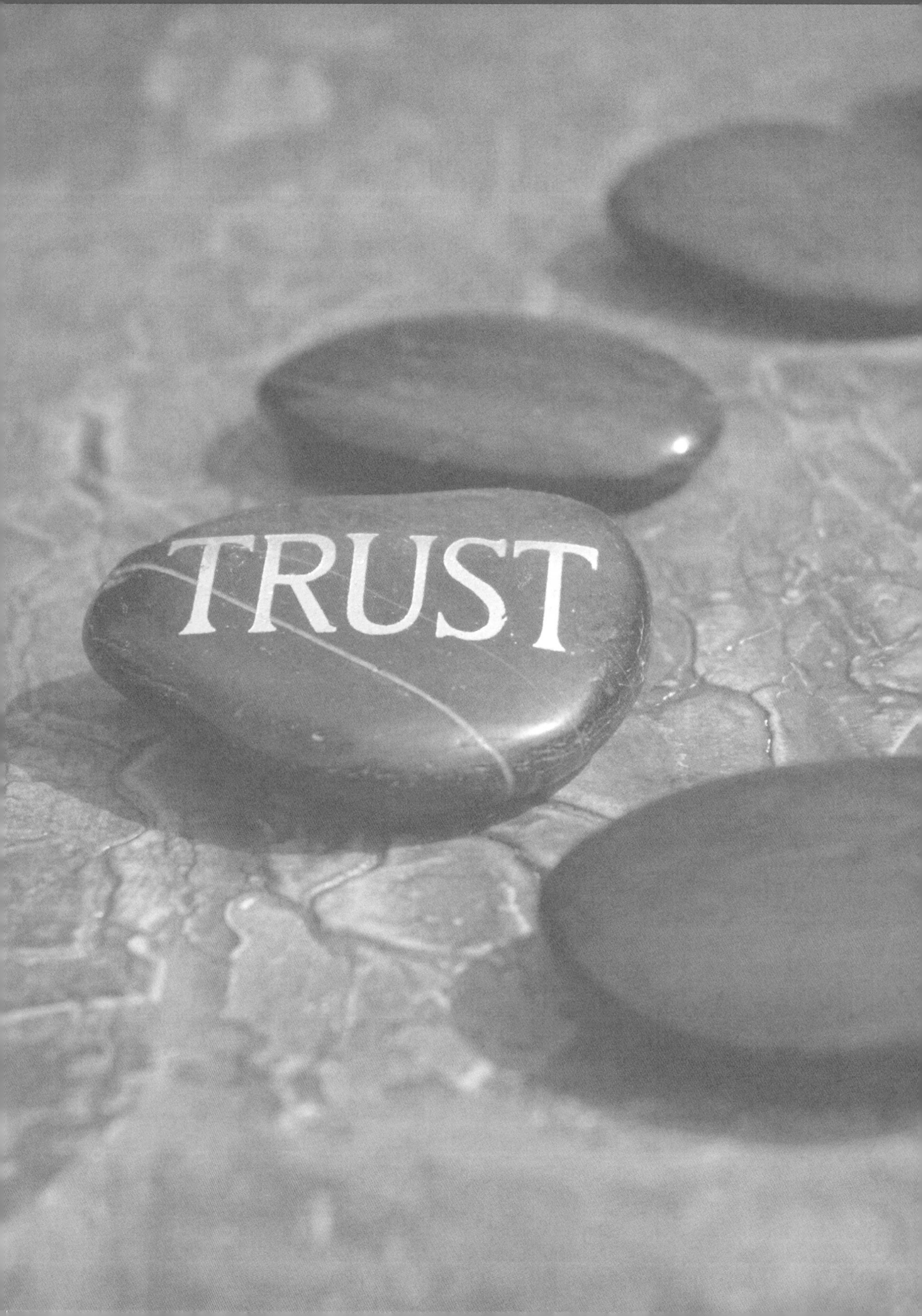
TRUST

"There is one thing that is common to every individual, relationship, team, family, organization, nation, economy, and civilization throughout the world — one thing which, if removed, will destroy the most powerful government, the most successful business, the most thriving economy, the most influential leadership, the greatest friendship, the strongest character, the deepest love. On the other hand, if developed and leveraged, that one thing has the potential to create unparalleled success and prosperity in every dimension of life. Yet it is the least understood, most neglected, and most underestimated possibility of our time. That one thing is trust."

— *S.M.R. Covey, 2008*

A s in most schools, the elementary school's teachers lounge was an active center for meeting and collegial conversation — and the place to find out the latest news on anyone and everything. So it was no surprise one day to walk in on a group of teachers with their heads huddled together, shooting glances over their shoulder as the door opened. As they continued their conversation, the gasps and whispers signaled that what they were saying probably wasn't going to be helpful to anyone. In fact, one teacher was sharing a destructive rumor about a colleague whose students had scored very well on a recent round of districtwide common assessments. The school's staff had begun analyzing these data in their professional

Developing trust requires coaches to take
on moral leadership and develop bonds
with those they coach in order to model
trust throughout the school.

learning teams. The allegation being made was that the teacher whose
students had done well had helped them cheat on the test. Of course, there
was no validity to the accusation; however, the teachers in the lounge
seemed to all agree and laughed. The school coach, who was present, didn't
dispute the rumor and joined in the laughter. As rumors do, this one spread
quickly. The coach even shared it with the principal's secretary. By the end
of the school day, emotional tension was high throughout the building. The
teacher who was being talked about also heard the rumor — and left the
building in tears.

As this story illustrates, coaches must be continuously guarded in their language
and actions. Coaches can be drawn into casual conversation and make comments
that violate trust. Trust, which often takes years to build, can be destroyed in seconds
without thought.

By intentionally focusing on trust, however, organizations and individuals can
endure fallout from everyday problems and more monumental crises. For example,
Isadore Sharp, founder, CEO, and chairman of the Four Seasons hotel chain,
attributes much of his organization's success to building trust with employees and
customers. "We can't communicate effectively across a trust gap. ... So I sat down with
our public relations director and detailed a formal credo based on the Golden Rule,
the cornerstone of what would be called our corporate culture" (Beslin & Reddin,
2006, p. 1).

Deloitte Canada, like many accounting firms, has had fallout from corporate
ethics scandals. In an e-conference of the Deloitte Leaders Forum in June 2005,
Deloitte Canada CEO Alan MacGibbon stressed the need for leaders to initiate
change and act decisively. "Trust is a concept that is so fundamentally important yet
so hard to define, earn, and keep," MacGibbon said. "Moral and ethical leadership is
perhaps the single most important contributor to success over the long haul" (Beslin &
Reddin, 2006, p. 1).

Stephen M.R. Covey (2008) described 13 trust behaviors: Talk straight, demonstrate respect, create transparency, right wrongs, show loyalty, deliver results, get
better, confront reality, clarify expectations, practice accountability, listen first, keep
commitments, and extend trust. The coach's role is to help leaders develop and model

PHOTO: KAY PSENCIK

Trustworthiness

Stop for a moment and think about the most trustworthy people in your life. How would you describe them to others?

The Treaty Oak, Austin, Texas

the character traits that lead to trusting relationships. And a coach's success in doing so depends on the coach's own trustworthiness. Developing trust requires coaches to take on moral leadership and develop bonds with those they coach in order to model trust throughout the school.

In the teachers lounge scenario, an effective coach, knowing her role and how trust was being violated, might have intervened. What might have been the outcome by the end of the day if the coach had asked the group of teachers some thoughtful questions: "I wonder if there is any real evidence that cheating took place? Is what we are talking about right now going to facilitate our working together well in the future or hinder it? What other conversations should we be having right now? I wonder what we could be learning from her classroom, or how her strategies and ideas might contribute to all of our learning?" The coach might have chosen many questions that would nurture and build trust in the organization, allow others to see the coach as trustworthy, and build positive energy in the organization.

As people focus energy and work on developing their own trustworthiness, they become like a mighty oak tree. A well-known tale in Austin, Texas, told on the city's website (www.ci.austin.tx.us/treatyoak/hist1.htmAustin), centers on an ancient grove of oak trees known as the Council Oaks that were, according to Native American legend, the location for launching war parties and for hosting peace treaties. Beneath one of these trees, Native Americans reportedly signed a treaty with settlers, represented by Stephen F. Austin. That tree now is known as the Treaty Oak. The Tejas tribe is said to have sat beneath it sipping tea made with honey and the tree's acorns.

In 1989, the tree was vandalized, poisoned with such a powerful hardwood herbicide that scientists were certain it would die. Lab tests showed the oak had received enough poison to kill 100 trees. However, the Treaty Oak survived. Eight years after the vandalism, in 1997, it once again produced a crop of acorns. City workers gathered and germinated the acorns, then distributed the seedlings throughout Texas. Two decades after the poisoning, the tree is thriving, although its shape is a reminder of its struggle to survive. Many Texans see the Treaty Oak as a symbol of strength and endurance.

Like the Treaty Oak, good coaches remain constant, symbols of strength and endurance through life's vicissitudes. People who understand their values and what is important to them are able to nurture relationships. But to build the trust that sustains relationships over time, coaches work to develop at least six traits based on the work of Daniel Goleman (2002), Megan Tschannen-Moran (2004), Julio Olalla (2003b), and Stephen Covey (2008).

The six trusty oak roots

A "trusty oak" coach has six essential deep roots: self-awareness, honesty, sincerity, competence, reliability, and the ability to be other-centered.

SELF-AWARENESS

Effective coaches have a deep sense of their own values and live by those values in such a way that others cannot doubt their principles. In *The Learning Educator* (2007), Stephanie Hirsh and Joellen Killion state, "Each person lives by a set of principles. Some of our principles are unquestioned and fundamental to who we are. Some are new to us, and through our experiences and dialogue we continue to clarify and deepen our understanding of them. Our principles guide our work, thoughts, goals, actions, and decisions" (p. 11). Dennis Sparks (2007) says we become clearer about who we are by making clear our assumptions in writing and by talking with others about them. Effective coaches spend time reflecting on and articulating the principles that guide their actions and attitudes. When self-awareness is practiced regularly as a skill, it becomes an essential part of the coach's character.

HONESTY

In a training session on strategic planning, administrators in the group were discussing how they shared district student performance data with the public. One participant said he struggled with sharing data when the news was not good. The facilitator, without much thought, agreed.

Then a superintendent spoke up. "Is it really difficult to tell the truth?" he asked.

Although the facilitator and the administrator may have been referring to the challenges of sharing bad news, the superintendent who spoke out never forgot the

The six trusty oak roots

Self-awareness
- What drives me? What inspires me?
- What values guide my actions?
- What contributions do I want to make to the world?
- What is my purpose for living?

Honesty
- How does what I think, do, and say align with my observations of the world?

Sincerity
- How do I act intentionally on my values?

Competence
- What do I do so well that I am credible to others?
- What attitudes and aspirations do I have that inspire me to learn continuously?
- What effect does the technological, global world in which we live have on my competence?
- What results am I most proud of?

Reliability
- What do I do to ensure I keep my promises?
- What do I do when I fail to keep my promises?

Intentions
- When I am with others, am I truly interested in them and what they have to say?
- Do I genuinely want the best for others on my team and regularly acknowledge their contributions?

CORES OF CREDIBILITY

Stephen Covey emphasizes building trustworthiness through four cores of credibility:

- **Integrity:** Are you congruent?

- **Intent:** What's your agenda?

- **Capabilities:** Are you relevant?

- **Results:** What's your track record?

Source: Covey, 2008.

facilitator's comment. She lost his trust, and he subsequently dismissed all she had to say.

Building trusting relationships is not about how honest we think we are. It is how honest others believe us to be. Truth releases the power of positive change. We build meaningful, healthy relationships and become positive role models for others through self-examination and being honest with ourselves and others.

SINCERITY

In today's fast-paced world, it is tempting to overcommit and make promises we do not really want to keep. When we hastily respond to an e-mail on the computer, glance furtively at a cell phone message, or jot a note on a to-do list when with another person, we are not totally focused or present, and that is obvious to the listener. Distractions keep our minds floating from issue to issue and cut our conversations short. The pressures of pending commitments keep us from listening. Effective coaches are truly present in the moment.

Sincerity requires that people follow through on those actions that they really are committed to doing. They plan and schedule appropriate time for those tasks they want to make their priorities.

Praise is another challenge to developing sincerity. When praise is not grounded, others may view it as insincere. "You are great!" and "You do fantastic work!" are examples of unspecific praise. When comments are unconnected to a particular event, others may think, "She always says that, but she has no idea what we do." Beware the habit of giving false praise.

COMPETENCE

Competent people inspire trust. Competent people have the skills, attitudes, and dispositions to achieve what they say they can. Taking on challenges outside one's area of expertise can be tempting, but staying focused in one's area of competence is essential to having others pay attention to the coach or leader and to feel confident in the leader. The coach's competence gives others the courage to act.

Aggressive learners are most likely to be viewed as competent. As Eric Hoffer states: "In times of drastic change, learners inherit the Earth, while the learned find themselves beautifully equipped to work in a world that no longer exists" (2008, p. 32). Competence is developed through continuous learning.

RELIABILITY

The root of reliability is the most easily severed as people attempt more in limited time. Those who are reliable can be counted on to keep their promises. Samuel Hamlin chose to participate in a three-year principal development coalition. In three years, he never missed a session. When his children were sick or he had a crisis at school, he found someone to help him so that he honored his commitment.

At the last session, he seemed tired. The leader asked if he was OK. Hamlin replied, "I am tired. I attended my aunt's funeral yesterday, and I've driven all night to be here this morning." Hamlin's commitments were meaningful to him.

Administrators often find themselves in a meeting running overtime or caught by someone who just has to talk, or lost in a phone call with an angry parent. While these may be excuses for not meeting a commitment, they are not reasons. No matter how many apologies are given, others' recall of the situation will be the failure to honor a commitment.

Phil Blake, president of Bayer, said, "It's all about authenticity ... plus consistency that you will always perform according to the contract of understanding. You're doing the right things for the right reasons and what's best for all" (Beslin & Reddin, 2006, p. 30).

Effective coaches honor others as they would want to be honored. When coaches are transparent, honest,

Pause and reflect

Think about your view of those with whom you interact. How might you have discounted others because you thought their intentions or motives were suspect or you believed their agenda was self-centered?

ASSUMPTIONS

» Effective coaches have a deep sense of who they are and build trusting relationships because they are honest, sincere, competent, and reliable.

» The most effective coaches are other-centered. They focus on others' successes without expecting personal recognition or gain.

and forthright with issues they are facing, others grow more confident they are what they say they are and that they can be counted on.

INTENTIONS

Highly effective coaches have the best intentions for those they coach. They accept people for who they are — brilliant, wonderful gifts to the planet — and want them to succeed. Jim Meehan, British psychologist and poet, puts it this way: "Having spent many years trying to define the essentials of trust, I arrived at the position that if two people could say two things to each other and mean them, then there was the basis for real trust. The two things were 'I mean you no harm' and 'I seek your greatest good' " (Covey, 2008, p. 80). The best coaches' motives are other-centered.

Taxes and dividends

Trust takes time to earn and can be destroyed almost instantly. Covey uses the idea of taxes and dividends to explain. Positive, high levels of trust in relationships with others and in organizations produce joy, effortless communication, transparent relationships, and high levels of energy — dividends. Organizations with low trust relationships have unhealthy working environments, hostility, guarded communication, defensiveness, and constant worry and suspicion (Covey, 2008, pp. 22-24). Feeding trust results in greater dividends, while mistrust taxes everyone and has long-term costs to relationships. Effective coaches strive to constantly earn dividends with those they coach.

Covey outlines four ways leaders build dividends:

1. **Inspire trust.** Believe in others' capacity to live up to expectations, to deliver on promises, and to achieve clarity on key goals. Avoid micromanaging and second-guessing.

2.   **Clarify purpose.** Involve others in creating the goals to be achieved. When people are involved in the process, they psychologically own the goals and share the mission, vision, and values.

3.   **Align systems.** Match what is said to what is measured. Organizations often claim, for example, that people are important but have structures and systems that identify professional learning as an expense or cost rather than an asset and investment in their people.

4.   **Unleash talent.** Empower others by aligning systems and developing a shared purpose. When people feel empowered, the organization benefits from their capacity, intelligence, creativity, and resourcefulness.

REFLECTIONS

Consider each of the trusty oak roots. How do you reflect these characteristics? What are your strengths? What have others shared with you about trusting you? Think about your areas of challenge. What actions would you take to strengthen that part of the root?

How can you live with greater transparency so that others see the authentic you? Think about living in transparency. What joys would you experience? How would that change affect your energy? What new emotions would you experience? What new language might you use? Explore your rationale for being unwilling to live in greater transparency. What are your energy levels around these aspects of your life? What are your emotions? What doors are closed because of your lack of transparency?

Consider others in your life for whom you intend the best. How do you listen to them? What questions do you ask? What support do you give them? Notice your body language and emotions when you are around them. What is your energy level? What is your attitude when you anticipate being with them? While you are with them?

STRATEGIES AND INVESTIGATIONS

» Read Stephen M.R. Covey's book, *The Speed of Trust* (Free Press, 2008). Find yourself and your organization on the dividend and tax tables. Establish one action that will move you closer to high-yield dividends in both your organization and your relationships with others.

» Create a trust pyramid. Write your greatest challenge at the top of the pyramid and your greatest strengths in building trusting relationships at the foundation of the pyramid. List actions you can take to turn your challenge to a foundational strength. Share your ideas with your study team or your own coach. Write an action plan and follow it.

» Renew a relationship. Make a list of people whose trust you may have violated and with whom you wish to renew your relationship. Establish a plan of action to use honesty and sincerity to renew the relationship. Decide how to approach this person. With a coach or observer, practice the conversation you want to have. Follow through, then reflect on the experience. Though this strategy is challenging, it can strengthen you as a coach — you may need to ask others to renew relationships.

» Practice being other-centered. Call someone you have not talked with in a while and be fully present for that person. When you become anxious about the time, note your body language and refocus on the other person. Give yourself permission to enjoy the conversation. Make notes afterward of signs that you were drifting, what strategies helped you refocus, and what you learned about yourself. Set a time to practice again. Keep notes in your journal about your efforts and the results of being present.

"I am of the opinion that my life belongs to the whole community, and as long as I live, it is my privilege to do for it whatever I can."

— George Bernard Shaw, Irish literary critic,
playwright and essayist

A coaching spirit is one of optimism, hope, and confidence. Through the skills they gain and the character traits they strengthen as they work, coaches gain a perspective and wisdom that enriches them and enables them to benefit those with whom they work.

Coaches, particularly those who work with leaders, have spirits that understand the coherence of body, mind, and language, that value life balance, that are sensitive to how humans learn, and that continuously strive for personal mastery. Beyond their skills and character, effective coaches' qualities of spirit make them not just good colleagues, but good people.

Effective coaches stop those they coach from
repeating the same story or allowing the same
mental tape to play again and instead help them
make new assessments, consider new solutions,
and build new mental models.

Changing mental models

Research has found that repeated actions create the same neuron firings in the brain, forming deep connections and pathways. The brain is eager to hardwire learning and move on to new information. Bloom (1986) called this process "automaticity." Through chunking and automaticity, the brain is able to put many functions on a sort of autopilot — allow the conscious brain to take on new tasks that demand attention while the automatic brain operates to make sense of new information. Pianists who have mastered playing the piano can concentrate on musicality, then, and not on reading each note. Dancers can focus on rhythm rather than the position of their feet. Golfers can strategize the game rather than think about their swing. This brilliant brain processing is much like a river that continues to flow over the same path for millions of years. It eventually carves out a Grand Canyon.

Though this hardwiring helps learned skills become automatic, it also results in mental models that become set in our brains. Consequently, adults have very thick lenses formed from years of hardwiring. "Mental models," Peter Senge says, "are deeply ingrained assumptions, generalizations, or even pictures or images that influence how we understand the world and how we take action" (1994, p. 8).

We see the world through our mental models — through the glasses we wear. If our mental model is that there is no hope for peace in the world, we will put out little effort to build peace. If our mental model is that children are lazy, we accept underperformance.

People tend to fight for and hold on to their views of the world, according to Rock (2006). "The brain truly sees the world according to its own wiring," he writes (p. 28). "In fact, the majority of the time, it's even worse than that — our brains will go to great pains to vehemently defend our existing mental models even to the point, at times of death."

Olalla (2003b) says, "Most people believe that human beings have the capacity to see things objectively. Basically, we assume that we all perceive the world around us in the same way. … We tend to argue about what we know to be true rather than consider

FIGURE 6.1 **Mental models**

Our views of the world are shaped by basic brain functions, our wants and needs, and our culture, experiences, and belief systems.

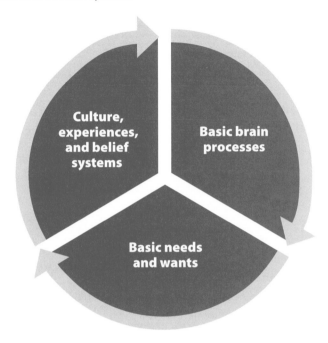

the possibility that there is more to know or that there is another way of seeing an issue" (p. 5).

Studies of crime witnesses bolster the view that people see the same situation differently. One significant study found that two-thirds of subjects failed to see a fight that they passed right by because they were focused on the jogger they were told to follow (Spiegel, 2011). Psychologists term this inattentional blindness, a human tendency to tune out what may be right in front of us while we focus on something else. Our own lenses create our individual reality. Our personal lenses also lead us to have difficulty seeing others' perspectives.

For coaches to facilitate others' learning, they must be aggressive learners themselves. As Rock stated, we all have mental models or maps that we have grown to believe are truths. Effective coaches model learning for their clients — they continuously work on opening opportunities for themselves, and they work to see the world through new lenses.

IMPLICATION FOR COACHING

A significant implication of brain research is for coaches to help those they coach create new mental models. Effective coaches question the principals they are coaching so that these leaders see things in ways they have never seen before, hear what they have never heard, and think in ways they have never thought. Effective coaches are skilled at leading generative, solution-centered conversations rather than problem-focused conversations. They are also most aware of their own mental models and guard against guiding those they coach to see the world as they see it.

Expert coaches help leaders beware of "tape playing." Telling our story to ourselves over and over again is like rewinding and repeatedly playing a tape in our brains. Mental models become more ingrained, more hardwired, like the same path repeatedly trodden. Effective coaches stop those they coach from repeating the same detrimental story or allowing the same mental tape to play again and instead help them make new assessments, consider new solutions, and build new mental models.

Coherence

He was paralyzed with fear.
She shouted for joy.
He embodied resignation.
She ripped him to shreds.
His words pierced her like arrows.

These sentences probably don't surprise anyone. We know, but often fail to recognize, that body, mind, and emotion are intricately connected. Brain science increasingly supports the idea that each of us is a tapestry — what affects our bodies affects our emotions and our language. What affects our emotions also affects our bodies. Our language and others' language directed toward us affects our bodies as well as our emotions. Each of us is a complete system that relies on coherence of the body, language, and emotion.

The brain is a complex parallel processor. Each human brain has the possibility of more than 100 billion neural firings, more than there are atoms in the universe (Hart, 1983). Unlike other animals, the human brain/mind is more than three-fourths cerebral cortex — the thinking brain.

Considering the whole-body context of emotions, the amygdala plays a significant role in choices that individuals make. The amygdala constantly scans the environment for dangers and threats. It regulates brain chemicals, and, under stress, releases adrenaline. Adrenaline is essential when humans fear for their lives, but the human system is not built for repeated flight-or-fight response. Living under continuous stress negatively impacts the body and can eventually kill.

The field of neuroscience recognizes this mind-body connection.

"Disease now is more chronic and related to behavioral and social processes," according to John T. Cacioppo, professor of social neuroscience at the University of Chicago (Dess, 2001). "So learning how stress, dietary habits, socioeconomic status,

*Effective coaches know the significance
of developing balance in life and lead
others to recognize and reduce the harmful
accumulations of stress in their lives.*

and other psychosocial factors affect the body and brain is moving up the health research agenda."

Emotion is inseparable from the body's limbic system. Candace Pert, a neuroscientist who has held a variety of research positions with the National Institute of Mental Health, notes that emotions are a complete experience — involving body, mind, and brain. Pert was among the earliest to point out that emotions involve both the body's limbic system and the mind's perceptions.

"The word 'trauma' has been used to describe both physical and mental damage," according to Pert. "People have a hard time discriminating between physical and mental pain. So often we are 'stuck' in an unpleasant emotional event — a trauma — from the past that is stored at every level of our nervous system and even on the cellular level — i.e., cells that are constantly becoming and renewing the nervous system. My laboratory research has suggested that all of the senses, sight, sound, smell, taste and touch, are filtered, and memories stored, through the molecules of emotions, mostly the neuropeptides and their receptors, at every level of the bodymind" (Pert, 1997, p. 142). The term bodymind defines the coherence and interrelationship among our bodies, minds, emotions, health, and well-being.

What that interrelationship means for how we experience others is clear.

A principal reached the end of a long day and was standing near the buses as students loaded. As she waited, a teacher approached her tentatively. She acknowledged the teacher, who had been a leader in the school but now seemed hesitant and even timid. "Are you angry at the staff?" the teacher asked. The principal was shocked. "Absolutely not!" she replied. She said couldn't be prouder of the teachers. The teacher told her, "We've all felt tension in the air, and we thought it must be us — that we were doing something wrong or somehow making you angry." After reflecting on that assessment, the principal recognized that she had not been able to cover up how sick she'd been feeling. She went to the doctor that day. She had mononucleosis that needed immediate and significant treatment.

Those who understand the importance of personal development and who have cultivated a high degree of personal mastery are most skilled at maneuvering through challenging times.

Body language can be louder than words. Those who feel nothing is right with their lives often manifest those feelings in a heavy step as they walk or in sluggish movements. Optimism shines through other people's voices and shows in the way they carry themselves.

Bodies mirror emotions. When a person is excited and energized, the body shows up animated. When someone is troubled, sad, angry, or fearful, the body takes on that emotion. The molecules of emotion integrate what we feel at every level of our "bodymind." Our bodies are our subconscious mind.

Effective coaches understand this coherence of body, language, and emotions. They are great observers of their own emotions and body when working with others and are sensitive to the impact they are having.

IMPLICATION FOR COACHING

Principals who take their work very seriously often are caught in constant turmoil, which may have a negative impact on their body and language. If the leader is prone to negative thoughts and has cultivated this mood over time, the school community may have adopted a mood of resignation or resentment toward their principal or colleagues, toward central office innovations, or even resentment toward students for not behaving or performing better. A school family also can embody an even greater challenge — resignation that things will never be better.

Brain theorists note that when a human being is afraid, the brain downshifts to the functions of the fight-or-flight brain. Powerful chemicals — noradrenaline, adrenaline, and cortisol — are released, and emotion dominates cognition. The rational brain gives way to the amygdala in a process sometimes called an "amygdala hijack" (Goleman, 1995). Learning is impeded.

Highly effective coaches carefully observe those they coach for coherence. Effective coaches note obvious signals from those they are coaching — their body language and their verbal signals. The coach may discover the need to work on the body or to address language that would lead the person being coached to a different emotion. They coach leaders to use different strategies connected to body, language, and emotions to help them achieve their goals.

The coach might suggest, "Let's try saying what you just said again. This time, I want you to use different body language for that comment. What if you stand up straight, hold your chin up a little, and put your shoulders back? Now say what you were saying. What new language comes up? What new emotions?" Or, the coach might say, "I understand you are feeling anger. What if you chose another emotion? How would you relate to that person? How would you benefit?"

Life balance

The coach was working with a group of principals learning coaching skills. The group had discussed and practiced the skills of listening, being present, questioning, and envisioning. As the coach sat back and observed, she saw clearly that tension in the room was high. Using Glasser's list (see p. 73), she asked the team members to write down how each of them satisfied his or her basic needs for power, belonging, freedom, and fun. The exercise took longer than she had anticipated as the group struggled. As the principals began to share, they all said they felt they had freedom in their jobs and were good leaders. They agreed they had few ideas to satisfy their need for belonging.

Only one person had written anything under "fun."

They loved their families but regretted not being with them much. They often felt guilty about taking care of other children and spending less time with their own. They told stories of how they used to love to play tennis, the piano, sing in the church choir, jog with their spouse, or to go to their children's soccer games. As active principals, they laughed about eating crackers on the run for lunch and drinking caffeine all day for energy. They shared that although they wanted to coach, they were not sure they could make another commitment and do the work well.

These leaders needed balance in their lives. Their mental models were not allowing them to see possibilities.

In *Living in Balance,* Joel Levey and Michelle Levey (1998) note that those who understand the importance of personal development and who have cultivated a high degree of personal mastery are most skilled at maneuvering through challenging times. They have learned to recognize when they are drifting out of balance. As a result, they are more likely to eat when they are hungry and to rest and renew themselves when they are tired.

Developing the mindfulness necessary to recognize and master stress also deepens the mind-body-spirit connection. Balance gives us the inner strength and understanding to meet every situation in a more centered way. A balanced life is reflected in a higher degree of self-confidence, self-control, self-acceptance, and self-respect. Effective coaches know the significance of developing balance in life and lead others to recognize and reduce the harmful accumulations of stress in their lives.

Practitioners of personal mastery share these characteristics:

» They have a sense of purpose behind their goals.

» Their vision is more like a calling than a good idea.

» They see current reality as an ally, not an enemy.

» They are committed to seeing reality increasingly accurately.

» They are extremely inquisitive.

» They do not resist, but work with, the forces of change.

» They feel connected to others and to life itself.

» They feel that they are part of a larger creative process that they can influence but cannot unilaterally control.

Source: Senge, 1994, pp. 139-173.

IMPLICATION FOR COACHING

Effective coaches guide leaders to commit not only to learning goals that affect school achievement, but also to value physical, social, emotional, and spiritual development in their lives.

They lead those they coach to become "balance masters," choosing options such as frequent exercise to manage stress and practicing self-renewal and revitalizing skills.

Personal mastery

Personal mastery means "continually clarifying and deepening our personal vision, of focusing our energies, of developing patience, and of seeing reality objectively," according to Senge (1994, p. 7).

The journey toward personal mastery is a commitment to explore how language, emotions, and body open — or close — opportunities to learn. This exploration leads us to discover how we think, feel, speak, and behave. Self-knowledge, in turn, allows us to control our brains and bodies, to explore our mental models and our choices, and to take charge of our own experiences.

Personal mastery is about creating what we want in our lives and work. Senge states, "Personal mastery goes beyond competence and skills. … It means approaching one's life as a creative work, living life from a creative as opposed to a reactive viewpoint" (1994, p. 141). According to Senge, continually expanding personal mastery is a discipline based on key principles and practices:

- Establishing a personal vision and goal for oneself;
- Determining a clear personal purpose;
- Holding creative tension between vision and current reality;
- Mitigating the impact of deeply rooted beliefs and mental models that are contrary to personal mastery; and
- A passionate commitment to truth (pp. 147-167).

"People with a high level of personal mastery live in a continual learning mode. They never 'arrive,' " Senge states (1994, p. 142). "Sometimes, language, such as the term 'personal mastery,' creates a misleading sense of definiteness, of black and white. But personal mastery is not something you possess. It is a process. It is a lifelong discipline. People with a high level of personal mastery are acutely aware of their ignorance, their incompetence, their growth areas. And they are deeply self-confident. Paradoxical? Only for those who do not see the journey is the reward."

Just as Senge says mental models determine individual realities, Hall (2000) contends that personal development is based on cognition: Thoughts determine truths and act as filters for our senses. Hall says it is not experiences that are significant but the meaning we give to those experiences. Personal mastery is the process of accessing our higher thoughts and feelings to evaluate our primary thoughts and feelings so that we can effectively choose those that serve us best. When we are able to evaluate our own thoughts, we can think about what we are thinking. We begin to ask ourselves metacognitive questions such as, "Is this way of thinking and feeling useful to me? What does it say about me that I am having these emotions and thoughts? What meanings am I associating with this situation? Are there other assessments of this situation that I could make that would be more useful to me?"

According to George Leonard, mastery is not a destination, but a journey. In *Mastery* (Penguin Books, 1991), Leonard shares the principles of the Zen master who taught his students the skill of patience in developing personal mastery. He shared that when learning comes too easily and without sufficient practice, students do not develop the persistence mastery requires. Mastery is a purposeful process by which things that seemed difficult or even impossible grow easier through practice.

The word *practice* is best conceived of as a noun, not as something one does, but as something a person has, something one is. Practice in this sense is akin to the Chinese word *tao*, which means, literally, road or path. Practice is the path upon which one travels. A practice (as a noun) can be anything practiced on a regular basis as an

---

THE ENGAGED LEARNER

Hall outlines strategies essential for mastery in adult learners. He states that the engaged learner:

- Restructures mind and emotions;

- Develops awareness of self-sabotaging frames;

- Recognizes his or her innate genius for personal and interpersonal development;

- Develops a passion for the excellence of expertise; and

- Recognizes the powerful mind-muscle connection for greater congruency.

Source: Hall, 2000, p. 265.

integral part of life — not in order to gain something else, but for its own sake. It might be a sport or the practice of medicine. It might be gardening or bridge or yoga or meditation, or it might be the practice of leading schools effectively.

For coaches, mastery may be a lifelong journey of continuous improvement. The master's journey requires diligent practice and effort to hone our skills, to attain new levels of competence. But we also have to be willing to spend most of our time on a plateau, to keep practicing even when we seem to be getting nowhere, Leonard (1991, p. 15). Too many take little time for themselves to be on a master's journey and to learn new skills, strategies, and behaviors.

> A district administrator was visiting the superintendent to talk about how to help principals in the district improve their effectiveness. She had created a plan and was sharing several learning strategies she thought the principals could engage in to increase their ability to create and lead high-performing schools. She pulled out a bibliography and mentioned book studies.
>
> The superintendent looked at her, then turned around to look at his bookshelf. He gestured toward a full shelf and said, "I've read every one of those books, and they haven't made any difference at all in my leadership."
>
> The professional developer barely stopped herself from blurting, "That's obvious!"

Malcolm Gladwell (2008) in his book, *Outliers,* examines the common attributes of highly successful individuals across many fields. Their common trait? Practice. "The idea that excellence at performing a complex task requires a minimum level of practice surfaces again and again in studies of expertise," he writes (pp. 39-40). "In fact, researchers have settled on what they believe is the magic number for true expertise: 10,000 hours."

IMPLICATION FOR COACHING

When coaches view themselves as continuous learners, they are models for others. When they work toward personal mastery, they have a vision of themselves as learners, and they clearly articulate their goals.

The mental mastery involved in "running your own brain" involves a discipline of understanding and skill. As in any field, when people master a set of competencies, they practice them tenaciously in authentic learning situations. Effective coaches lead those they coach to run their own brains and to use a variety of metacognitive strategies to assist them.

Understanding adult learners

The adult learner brings life experiences to learning. As adults mature, their self-concept moves from dependency to self-direction, and they accumulate their own resources through their growing reservoir of experiences (Knowles, 1973, 1975, 1984, & 1990).

Adults are autonomous and self-directed. They want to analyze their own problems and determine their own futures. They have accumulated life experiences and knowledge from education and work, family, and social interactions. They seek to connect their learning to their current knowledge and experience base. Adults tend to be goal-oriented. They perform at their best when they define their goal(s) for their learning. They seek relevancy. Their learning is more effective if what they are learning has immediate application to their work. Adults perform best when they feel respected as competent to solve their own problems.

Expert coaches understand that adults' thoughts and experiences vary widely according to their beliefs, values, knowledge, experiences, understandings, decisions, and ideas. "Thoughts" can take different forms through all our senses. As we assess our experiences, thoughts or mental models often get in the way of our achieving our goals. Negative thinking can get in the way: "I just can't do that!" "They won't let us!"

We can also jump levels and think about our "thoughts," termed metacognition. When we do, we layer one level of thinking upon another level. Metacognition creates challenges for the learning coach: How do we explore the multilevel, complex frames or mental models that make up who we are as learners? How do we capitalize on these frames to accelerate personal learning? How do we reflect on the mental models that are barriers to our learning and to establishing strategies for creating new mental models that facilitate our learning?

We know each of us creates our own reality, so we begin to think of ways we can approach learning for

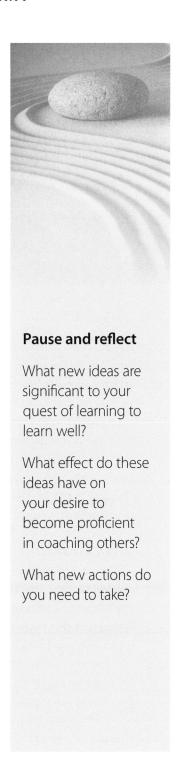

Pause and reflect

What new ideas are significant to your quest of learning to learn well?

What effect do these ideas have on your desire to become proficient in coaching others?

What new actions do you need to take?

> ## ASSUMPTIONS

» Our bodies, emotions, and language are coherent — that is, they are so integrated that what affects one affects all.

» Effective coaches model learning for those they coach.

» Learning creates new mental models.

» Principals who lead high-achieving schools are continuous learners.

» Those who lead balanced lives are full of energy, passion, gratitude, and joy. They exude optimism and hope.

ourselves. By seeing ourselves as though we already are what we envision ourselves to be, we work toward becoming our vision. Leaders in the field of personal development call this approach affirmation. We affirm what we want to become, and by doing so, we become that new image (Tice, 1989).

Coaches understand the power of affirmations and work with those they coach to establish affirmations that lead them to see themselves differently. If a leader wants everyone in the school to perceive him or her as a collaborative, visionary leader, the coach works with the leader to write and say regularly a statement similar to, "I am a visionary leader who works effectively and collaboratively with everyone in my school to achieve our vision."

IMPLICATION FOR COACHING

If coaches examine the adult learner, as defined by Knowles (1973), and compare coaching approaches, they discover that adults need to be independent and have a sense of control over their decisions. Successful coaches acknowledge the wealth of experiences that those they coach bring. Successful coaches lead those they are coaching to voice opinions freely and to discover for themselves what they want to achieve and how they are going to achieve it. Through coaching, the leaders can ground their strategies for achieving their goals through research and develop their understanding of systems thinking and effective change processes.

Another coaching consideration is that most leaders experience multiple setbacks. Coaches help those they are coaching develop competence in coping with living on the plateau and help them develop new ways of thinking or new skills to lead. Effective coaches help those they are coaching establish systems to practice their skills (reach that magic 10,000 hours), strategies for perseverance, systems to monitor their progress, systems for seeking and accepting feedback, and systems for celebrating progress.

Coaches as guides

Highly effective coaches see themselves as aggressive learners. They model what they want to see in others, have a deep understanding of how adults learn, seek coherence, live a balanced life, and are full of energy, passion, and gratitude. They focus on their gratitude for opportunities to serve others and commit to discovering the joy of being fully present each and every day. They set their own goals and help those they coach set goals, and develop skills and strategies for maintaining their enthusiasm.

Most important, they help those they coach connect their actions, attitudes, and commitments to life results. They guide those they coach to recognize their own and others' feelings, to develop strategies for motivating themselves, and to manage their bodies, emotions, and language. Knowing the coherence of body, emotions, and language, skilled coaches are great observers of others' bodies, emotions, and language. Through strategic questioning and envisioning, effective coaches guide those they coach to take responsibility for their lives and to live well.

REFLECTIONS

In what ways are you aware of the impact of your own mental models on the way you see the world, interact with others, and make decisions? In what ways do you guard against ungrounded mental models negatively impacting your interactions with others?

Think about the balance in your own life. What happens to your energy and joy when your life is out of balance? How do you work to maintain balance in your life?

How do you maximize your understanding of the coherence of your body, language, and emotions to work with others effectively?

Think back on a time when you were really excited, really happy. What was your language? What were your emotions? How did your body show up? Think back on a time when you were really ill. What impact did that have on your relationship with others? Your emotions? Your attitudes and your language?

Reflect on your strengths and understandings in each of the major concepts in this chapter: coherence, the adult learner, personal mastery, and the significance of a balanced life. What plan of action will you need to explore these concepts and understand them more deeply? Think of ways to apply these concepts and principles to your own life.

STRATEGIES AND INVESTIGATIONS

» Play a variety of music. Note how the music changes your emotion. Note your body. What shifts do you observe?

» Write an essay or poem about yourself. Contrast your moods and emotions. What about your mood supports your ability to coach others to lead high-performing schools? What gets in the way? What steps might you take to develop a mood to facilitate your success as a coach? Share your thoughts with a close friend. Write your reflections after the conversation.

» Consider how coaches develop the skills to lead others to practice learning. How do coaches help principals live on the plateau and engage in leading and learning? Make notes in your journal and refer to them as you continue to coach.

» In what ways do you or could you apply Senge's principle of personal mastery to your own life: "Personal mastery is the discipline of continually clarifying and deepening our personal vision, of focusing our energies, of developing patience, and of seeing reality objectively" (1994, p. 7). Write in your journal about your personal mastery strategies.

» Write notes in your journal about conversations in which participants are working toward personal mastery or reflect balance in their lives. What questions, aligned with adult learning theory, might you ask to strengthen their learning strategies?

» Make learning a top priority in your life. Become a possibilities thinker. Establish a challenging goal, and work to develop skills to remove barriers to achieve it.

STRATEGIES AND INVESTIGATIONS

» With a partner, practice body and emotion work. Look:
- Determined.
- Stable.
- Open to new ideas.
- Afraid.
- Uncertain.
- Courageous.
- Happy.
- Gloomy.
- Suspicious.

Give each other feedback. Did the body tell the story? Practice again. Try on different emotions than those listed. Practice body and emotion work by going to a difficult board meeting or meeting with a superintendent, holding a news conference about student performance data, calming a violent situation at school, facilitating professional learning with a challenging team. How will you walk in? Where will you sit? How will you hold your body posture? Your head? What emotion will you choose? Practice. Practice going before the media with a difficult situation. Practice firing someone. Practice a difficult conversation you need to have with your spouse, partner, child, parent, friend. What emotion do you need? What body posture is essential?- Reflect on your practice. What are you learning about the coherence of the body, emotions, and language? Write your observations and reflections in your journal.

» Consider areas where your life seems out of balance. Establish a plan of action to regain balance, and seek a coach's help. Reflect regularly on your progress. Record in your journal what you are learning about yourself.

» Plan a book study around Dennis Sparks' *Leading for Results* (Corwin Press & NSDC, 2007) and *Leadership 180* (Solution Tree, 2010) to inspire leaders to be continuous learners, reflective in their practice, clear about their values, and thoughtful about their learning.

RESOURCES FOR CHAPTER 6

Lieb, S. (1991, Fall). *Principles of adult learners.* Available online at www.honolulu.hawaii.edu/intranet/committees/FacDevCom/guidebk/teachtip/adults-2.htm.

Senge, P., Kleiner, A., Robert, C., Ross, R., & Smith, B. (1994). *The fifth discipline fieldbook: Strategies and tools for building a learning organization.* New York: Crown Publishing Group.

Senge, P., Kleiner, A., Roberts, C., Ross, R., Roth, G., & Smith, B. (1999). *The dance of change: The challenges of sustaining momentum in learning organizations.* New York: Doubleday.

Senge, P., Cambron-McCabe, N., Lucas, T., Smith, B., Dutton, J., & Kleiner, A. (2000). *Schools that learn: A fifth discipline fieldbook for educators, parents, and everyone who cares about education.* New York: Doubleday.

Symond, G. (2007, June). *Positive affirmation: A positive thinking technique.* Available online at www.vitalaffirmations.com/articles/why-positive-affirmations.htm.

Strategies of highly effective coaches

"Coaching is a supportive process for aligning the internal self with outer results. Coaches seek to bring out hidden abilities and help individuals live their lives on purpose, stemming from a clear picture of their strengths, values, and a sense of their personal mission."

— *Reiss, 2007*

"It is hard out there in the landscape of school leadership. It can be brutal and lonely work. Principals often feel vulnerable and insecure. Our research tells us that their outlook and attitudes about their profession run through cycles ranging from desperation to optimism. It is no surprise, then, that principals frequently turn to their coaches for empathy and reassurance in addition to professional support."

— *Bloom, Castagna, Moir, & Warren, 2005, p. 11*

A coach was visiting a highly skilled master principal who felt frustrated by the increasing demands and rigorous expectations that go with today's school leadership. Under pressure that might shatter the most competent CEO, this principal said to his coach, "I have learned to be a really great manager, but each time I learn more about creating an effective school and the strategies and skills principals need, I honestly feel like I am beginning my career again. I rarely feel confident that I can face whatever I need to face or know what I need to know to lead my school to be a high-performing community of learners."

Leading schools is complex. The most effective principals sometimes feel like beginners as they continuously move through stages of learning. Effective coaching requires matching coaching strategies with the leader's stage of learning and needs, and incorporates a variety of approaches in order to differentiate coaching, what some term blended coaching (Bloom, Castagna, Moir, & Warren, 2005).

Principals may at times require coaching that is more directive. For example, a new principal might ask for and need help designing a schedule for the staff's professional learning. A principal about to make a career-threatening decision needs the coach to be a mentor and facilitator. Principals whose personal lives are interfering with their professional lives need life coaches. A principal and coach might work together to determine the best way to help faculty improve student achievement, and the coach might then use a more facilitative approach. At times, the coach is purely questioning. Blended coaching draws on a number of coaching disciplines, including cognitive coaching (Costa & Garmston, 2002) and transformational coaching (Hargrove, 1995).

Different scenarios call for different strategies — or for coaches to blend a number of strategies within a single session. The distinctions emerging in the literature are coaches as *mentors, facilitators, collaborative/consultative* coaches, coaches for *personal mastery*, and coaches for *systems change*. Coaches who have the skills for each can readily move from one approach to another depending on the needs of the individual being coached. What is essential is for the coach to know the differences and to match the leader's needs with the appropriate strategy. Each strategy has a distinct purpose, an attitude or essential disposition required of the coach, and a set of essential skills.

Mentoring

Purpose	Disposition	Skills
To help the individual practice effective leadership skills.	• Respect for beginners and the skills, enthusiasm, and energy they bring to the job. • High expectations for success.	• Modeling. • Planning. • Next-step thinking. • Questioning.

When coaches mentor leaders, they must be careful not to build dependency. If the individual being coached comes to depend on solutions from the coach, the coach is not an effective coach.

New principals and assistant principals at the beginning of their careers might need mentoring, as might principals in trouble. Times when mentoring might be appropriate include: building a strategy for the beginning of school; planning an agenda for a parent advisory meeting; building a schedule that includes daily, embedded professional learning; or devising strategies to engage staff in analyzing student data.

Facilitative coaching

Purpose	Disposition	Skills
To help principals use constructivist strategies — those that guide the leader to create his or her own solutions (construct them) and to design his or her own plan of action.	The person I am coaching is capable of solving his or her own issues or achieving goals he or she has established.	• Questioning. • Evaluating for assessments and unfounded assertions. • Paraphrasing. • Observing. • Problem solving. • Giving effective feedback. • Reflective practices.

The coach's challenge is to stay facilitative and not become instructive or directive. A coach might use a facilitative approach when leaders are struggling with issues or problems that they have faced for a long time or when they continuously make ungrounded assessments, such as, "Teachers in my building will not participate in professional learning!" or "Parents at my school don't support their own children's learning or our school."

Collaborative/consultative coaching

Purpose	Disposition	Skills
To generate powerful learning for the individual being coached.	We are in this together.	• Problem solving. • Questioning. • Systems thinking. • Planning. • Envisioning.

The coach's challenge is to establish a partnership relationship, not to facilitate, but to work as co-collaborators. Collaborative coaching is best used when the coach and person being coached have identified a need or problem conducive to shared work, such as developing a schedule that includes common planning time for all teachers or helping a reluctant team use common assessments effectively.

Coaching for personal mastery

Purpose	Disposition	Skills
To assist principals with personal as well as professional issues.	Life is more than work. Because of the coherence of the body, emotions, and language, personal challenges may be interfering with professional success.	• Questioning. • Reflecting. • Giving feedback.

The coach's challenge is to remember that a coach is not a counselor; effective coaches know when to recommend counseling and when the individual being coached has presented issues the coach is not trained to help with.

This type of coaching might be useful with those leaders who have said such things as:

- "I'm really an introvert."
- "I don't have much confidence."
- "I rarely speak up at administrative staff meetings. When I do speak, I worry about what others will think."
- "I don't think my boss likes me. No matter what I share, I can't get his attention."
- "I feel like I am put down for my ideas."
- "I don't like one of my staff members!"
- "I'm struggling with high blood pressure."
- "I want to become a superintendent, but …"

Coaching for systems change

Purpose	Disposition	Skills
To coach not only the principal, but teacher leadership teams and possibly the entire staff and parents to create systems changes.	• I've done this before; I know how to organize systems; I have experience with this issue. • I can build leadership, shared vision, and plans to achieve powerful goals for students. • I have no fear. • You tell me it's a problem; I tell you we can work on it together.	• Systems thinker and designer. • Understanding of how to create a professional learning community. • Conflict resolution. • Vision building. • Data analysis. • Goal setting. • Program design. • Knowledge of change theory, logic models, curriculum and assessment design, and effective instruction.

The coach's greatest challenge with systems coaching is to coach and not to assume the principal's role. Another major challenge is to understand systems thinking, professional learning, and change theory well enough to help the principal uncover organizational breakdowns. Chapter 9 will discuss change theories and how to identify breakdowns.

The systems coaching approach might be useful when a school staff is continuously unsuccessful in achieving goals or when principals are placed in a challenged, underperforming school.

Determining an approach

In working with human beings, no one approach may be appropriate. Let's look at some case studies (in which the names have been changed) and consider coaching approaches.

> Ricardo Rodriguez is a creative, energetic, visionary assistant principal. He knows the impact he can have on improving student achievement. In five years of intensive work, he has transformed the staff's curricular and instructional decisions so that the school is off the state's low-performing list. The principal hired Rodriguez for his expertise and passion, but Rodriguez has discovered that his principal does not share that vision or expertise. Although the principal is willing to have Rodriguez take the lead in instruction, Rodriguez senses that the principal also resents the relationship developing between Rodriguez and the staff. Rodriguez also believes the principal often takes credit with the central office for what Rodriguez is doing. Rodriguez has interviewed for several principalships, only to find out that his principal recommended that Rodriguez be hired as a curriculum coordinator because of his knowledge of instruction and professional development, but said he was not ready for the principal's role.

In working with Rodriguez, the coach may begin with strategies for coaching for personal mastery. The coach may seek to find out what Rodriguez values and what is important to him. The coach might ask, "Is staying in the district more important than becoming a principal elsewhere? Do you want to achieve your current district's goals regardless of where you are working?" The coach also may choose to use mentoring strategies with Rodriguez to help him plan his next steps.

> Dashawna Webb, a skilled and experienced principal, was hired to lead a building undergoing major renovations, attention to which consumed her first two years of work in the building. She spent her time selecting cabinets and carpet rather than attending to instruction. Her staff saw her

as a great manager as the school operated smoothly, but Webb wants to be an instructional leader. She now spends time observing classrooms and attending collaboration sessions with the staff, and she has found the teachers have low expectations of students. She hears troubling comments, such as: "Well, you know where those children come from!" "We just can't expect every child to go to college." "Some of our children just are not prepared for school." The time required to manage the construction project drained Webb, and she now has health problems she does not want to make public. Webb doesn't know where to start to become the principal she aspires to be and to regain her health.

Webb is an experienced principal. The coach might best start with a facilitative approach. Through the coach's effective questioning strategies, paraphrasing, and maybe even scenario planning, Webb will create a new vision for her school, design a process to tackle the culture of low expectations she has noted, and design her own path to achieve her goal. There may be times when the coach may choose a more collaborative approach, as the coach may have much to learn from Webb, as well.

Dalton Woodward has been a principal for six years. He is well-read, creative, and smart. He builds great relationships with his staff, and the school climate survey results show that students, staff, and parents like the school very much. The challenge is student performance. Student achievement on the state standardized test has declined every year since he became principal. The school has been on the state's low-performing list for so many years that the state will restructure it next year. Woodward has shared with his coach that he wanted to be sure everyone was happy; now he wants to prove that he can raise student achievement even though he knows he will be removed as principal.

Woodward is a perfect candidate for systems coaching. The coach may approach Woodward about the opportunity to attend his leadership team meetings as a process observer. The coach may want to conduct a walk-through of the building and meet with groups of teachers to help Woodward determine the breakdowns in the system that have the greatest impact on student achievement. The coach may want to study trends in the school's data, observe teaching, attend collaborative sessions, and work with Woodward to identify the critical issues that impact low student performance.

Together with the leadership team, Woodward and the coach may develop a plan of action that would accelerate learning for all. The systems coach would be on-site often and help the teams reflect about their progress and determine essential new actions along the way until the school reaches its goals of high student performance.

ASSUMPTIONS

» Schools are complex organizations that require highly skilled leaders who are continuous learners, accept new challenges, maneuver unexpected events in their world, and implement with fidelity new national, district, or school innovations.

» Skilled coaches who match their coaching approach to leaders' needs will successfully help them accelerate their learning.

» The effective coach coaches for personal mastery to build self-confident learners who solve their own problems and create their own effective systems.

As a coach listens deeply and discovers the challenges a leader is facing, the coach moves fluidly among different coaching approaches. The coach facilitates the leader's learning to allow the leader to gain all the skills and confidence needed to lead.

REFLECTIONS

What are the key distinctions among the different approaches to coaching?

What approaches are most intriguing to you?

What do you want to learn more about?

Which approaches to coaching are your greatest strengths?

What do you wish to learn more about?

How do you want to go about learning those things?

STRATEGIES AND INVESTIGATIONS

» Reflect on the skills you are developing as a coach. What are your new strengths in coaching principals? What still challenges you? How might you address those concerns?

» As you have developed skills in coaching, how have your new skills affected those you coach? How will the different approaches to coaching shared in this chapter strengthen your coaching skills? What impact might those distinctions have on those you coach?

» What aha moments have you had while reading this chapter? What do you want to know more about?

» Use the following scenarios or the scenarios in this chapter to think about what coaching strategies you would use: mentoring, facilitative, collaborative, coaching for personal mastery, or systems coaching. Or use your own experiences from principals you know. Find a partner to play the role of the principal, and practice coaching that leader. After each practice session, reflect with your partner on the quality of your questions in helping the individual being coached to see the situation in new ways and discover new options.

  • Damira is an experienced principal who has worked in several schools. She is most proud that she and the staff have improved student achievement on standardized assessments. She, the staff, and her community have agreed that they need to broaden their definition of student success and incorporate workforce development skills into the curriculum. Damira is excited, but also worries that scores on standardized assessments will decline.

  • Erin, an experienced high school principal, made several students angry over disciplinary decisions. The students altered photos of her and made it appear she was entering a hotel room with a man not her husband, and they published the photos on the web. Although most of the students knew the pictures were fake, many who saw them on social media did not. Erin, humiliated, asked local police to investigate who posted the photos and wanted to press charges for slander.

  • Anja is a new principal who just completed her administrative certification. Her superintendent assigned her to a challenged school where no one else had been able to make a difference, convinced that Anja's enthusiasm would be key to a turnaround. The superintendent is convinced that if Anja will just do what he tells her, the school will succeed.

  • Andreas is a master principal eager to transform his school from a traditional to a student-centered high school. He envisions students taking classes determined not by time but by proficiency, students engaged in college courses long before traditionally expected, students working in internships in the community in areas of interest to them. The

STRATEGIES AND INVESTIGATIONS

administration and staff think Andreas should just follow district norms and not make waves.

- Nikhil is new to his school but is not new to the principalship. Nikhil has trouble building relationships, and faculty in the new school do not have a high opinion of him. Staff members believe he does not respect their work. He often talks about his superiority, how little teachers know about teaching, and how they are not willing to learn new strategies to ensure student success. He shares openly and regularly that the teachers don't want to do much work, they don't value education, don't think that students can learn, and won't listen to him or try what he wants them to. With an eye constantly on career advancement, Nikhil has decided to seek a superintendency.

- April is an experienced principal, but she has just been assigned to a new building that has had multiple principals over the last several years. Students are out of control, and teachers feel helpless. She resents being moved to "this place." She is openly critical of the school's staff, parents, and students. She wants to succeed, but is not sure she has the energy for this new environment.

Make notes in your journal about the kinds of questions that seem essential for the scenarios you selected. For example, what distinguishes a powerful question in a facilitative approach from a question in the collaborative/consultative approach?

» Ask principals in your area if you can practice coaching with them. Listen to them to determine their needs, then decide which of the five coaching strategies to use to help them develop their plans of action. Reflect with them about the coaching session. Tape these sessions if the leader will allow. Listen to the tapes, and reflect on the questions you asked, the coaching approaches you chose, and the leader's responses and actions. What are you learning about coaching? What would you have done differently? What were you most pleased about?

» Ask a fellow coach to listen in to your coaching session or to one of your taped sessions and to coach you as you reflect on your work.

» Observe other coaches' sessions or listen to tapes. Note the shifts the coaches make among mentoring, facilitative, collaborative/consultative, coaching for personal mastery, and systems coaching. What questions did the coach ask to shift responsibility for decision making to the individual being coached? What skills did you observe that you could you use? What would you have done differently?

RESOURCES FOR CHAPTER 7

Luecke, R. & Ibarra, H. (2004). *Coaching and mentoring.* Boston: Harvard Business School Press.

Reeves, D.B. & Allison, E. (2009). *Renewal coaching: Sustainable change for individuals and organizations.* San Francisco: Jossey-Bass.

Reiss, K. (2007). *Leadership coaching for educators: Bringing out the best in school administrators.* Thousand Oaks, CA: Corwin Press.

Underhill, B.O., McAnally, K., & Koriath, J.J. (2007). *Executive coaching for results: The definitive guide to developing organizational leaders.* San Francisco: Berrett-Koehler Publishers.

Weingartner, C.J. (2009). *Principal mentoring: A safe, simple, and supportive approach.* Thousand Oaks, CA: Corwin Press & NSDC.

Young, P.G., Sheets, J.M., & Knight, D.D. (2005). *Mentoring principals.* Thousand Oaks, CA: Corwin Press.

"Through language, we not only describe what is real for us, but we generate a world of possibilities, we make events happen, we create our identity and we coordinate actions with others."

— *Olalla, 2003a*

Some contend that what distinguishes humans from most mammals is language. Through our evolution, we have developed skills in managing our world, getting what we want, and working with others by using language. Watching infants develop language is a joy and a reminder of the power of words. We often hear parents of small children saying, "Use your words to get what you want, not your emotions."

Effective use of language corresponds to effective action. "Viewing language as generative opens up an important field of learning," says Julio Olalla. "If we improve our ability to communicate, we can substantially increase our effectiveness, our coordination of actions with others, our personal well-being, and our personal power" (2000, p. 1).

Speech acts allow us to coordinate action. Many administrators early in their careers find it challenging to coordinate action among all who have tasks to complete effectively for everyone to achieve their goals. When we coordinate action effectively, we get work done successfully and meet everyone's conditions of satisfaction. Leaders often find themselves overburdened with work and think their only option is to work longer, faster, and harder. Olalla makes these distinctions clear. Distinguishing among assessments and assertions, requests, declines, promises, offers, and establishing conditions of satisfaction are essential to coordinating action.

Effective coaching requires that coaches be aware of their language and listen carefully to the way those they coach use language to get work done or coordinate actions.

Assessments and assertions

We seldom speak using precise facts. We may use facts to make a point about our understanding of the way the world operates, but simply stating facts makes for a relatively boring conversation. For example, we rarely say to schools, "Your test scores in 2008 show that 75% of 3rd graders did not meet the state standard for passing." Such statements are assertions — these are facts that the listener could look at published data to verify. When we hear such an assertion, we immediately make judgments — or assessments — about that school, the staff, and the students:

- "These students are not learning to read."
- "Teachers are not teaching 3rd-grade students the standards effectively."
- "These students will not be successful in 4th grade."
- "The principal does not focus enough attention on student learning."

These interpretations of the data are based on our experiences and culture. We live in a world of assessments. In Houston, Texas, when the temperature is around 60 degrees, those who live there think it is very cold. Someone who is visiting Houston from northern British Columbia, on the other hand, thinks 60 degrees is great weather. Assessments are based on individual experiences and perspective.

Effective coaches are constantly aware of how a principal's assessment of an issue may be causing a breakdown and interfere with the principal's goals. It might be the principal's thoughts; it might be the data. For example:

The students are sluggish entering school every morning; they hang out in the cafeteria and ignore the signal to move to class. The breakdown: Instruction does not start on time.

Teachers are using collaboration time to discuss children misbehaving. The breakdown: Teams are not analyzing student work and making instructional decisions.

The principal's assessment is that not all teachers are engaged in developing common assessments. The breakdown: Common assessments are not ready for teams to use when discussing student progress.

The coach helps the principal ground assessments with assertions. For example, a leader might say: "Teachers just won't want to participate in professional development." "The teachers won't engage in school planning." "The kids are lazy and don't want to learn." "Poor parents just don't care about their children's education." "The school board won't let us." Hearing these assessments, the coach helps the leader consider assertions — whether data and facts support the statements and whether the data are sufficient evidence to deem the assessment to be true. For example, when a principal says, "Teachers just won't want to participate in professional development," a coach might ask: "What data do you have to support this assessment of your teachers? What observations have you made that lead you to this conclusion?"

Declarations and requests

Other distinctions are between declarations and requests. Declarations are clearly articulated expectations. Any response to a declaration results in consequences. For example, if a teacher declares to a student that the child should finish the assignment before going out to recess, the implication is clear that if the student does not finish the assignment, she will not have recess. If principals declare that all teachers will be outside their door during passing time, and one teacher is not, there is a consequence for that teacher. Requests, however, allow for the possibility that the person may decline the request without consequences. The requester must be ready to accept any outcome. For example, if the teacher says instead, "Will you be able to finish your assignment before recess?" the child may not complete the work and still may go to recess. The teacher accepts that response and the child's behavior.

Requests carry with them the opportunity for others to say no or to decline without repercussions, as in this conversation:

Principal: "Would you be willing to organize the strategic planning process for our school?"

Teacher: "No, I am not willing to do that at this time. Thanks for considering me."

Principal: "Thanks. I'll ask you for something else in the future."

End of conversation. Since there are no consequences, the teacher does not need to explain further. He only has to say, "No, thank you."

Since the principal made a request, she should not beg the teacher to reconsider.

Coaches help principals to understand the differences and how to make clear to their staffs, students, and parents whether they are making a declaration or request. Many people intend to make a declaration, but speak in request form. Although the speaker does not mean to allow for choice, that fact is concealed by the form of the language, leaving the listener confused. Principals might confuse their message by saying, "Would you all please be sure to be on time to your classrooms?" "Would you please be at your duty station at lunch?" "Would you please get your lesson plans in on time?" However, they mean, "Do this! If you do not, I am going to take note, and we are going to have a different conversation."

A declaration is straightforward: "I expect you to be at your duty stations at lunch." "I expect to see your lesson plans in on time." "We will all implement the strategies outlined in our school plan. Failure to do so will result in …"

Worse are those who use sarcasm as declaration: "Doesn't anyone ever see that the trash can is full?" The obvious answer is, "No." Or the leader says, "I'm the only one who seems to be on duty at lunch!" The confused listener doesn't know whether this is a declaration, a request, or merely an observation.

Knowing the distinctions between declarations and requests and using these speech acts purposefully greatly increases our effectiveness in interactions with others. Highly skilled coaches may ask those they coach:

- What declarations do you need to make?
- What requests have you made that really are declarations?
- What next steps do you want to take to clear up the confusions others are experiencing because they assumed your language was a request?
- What requests do you need to make of others?
- Can listeners say no without consequences?

Promises and offers

Promises have as much to do with trust as with coordinating action. When we promise to fulfill a request, the person making the request believes we will follow through. They no longer think of finding someone to do what was asked. A promise conversation might look like this:

Principal: "Will you facilitate the school's strategic planning effort this year?"
Teacher: "I would love to."
Principal: "Great! Thanks. Let's have a planning meeting next Thursday at 4 p.m. Is that acceptable?"
Teacher: "Fine with me!"

But at 4 p.m. Thursday, when the principal is waiting in her office, the teacher does not show up. His failure to fulfill a promise leads to frustration, anger, work not completed, and organizations in disarray. Stephen M.R. Covey (2008) notes, "Beginners are many; finishers are few. Increasingly, it seems, we live in a society of victims and quitters. ... My motto is, whenever possible, finish, and finish strong" (p. 123). In other words, trustworthy people keep their promises.

In coordinating actions effectively, promises to fulfill a commitment are essential to school success.

Principal: "Will you facilitate the school's strategic planning effort this year?"
Teacher: "I would love to consider it. I would like to know more about the job. What are your expectations? What do you hope our school can accomplish with a

FIGURE 8.1 The dance

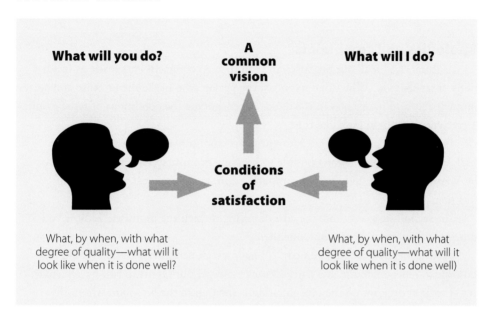

strategic plan? What would the expectations be of me? What would quality facilitation look like to you? What time commitment am I making?"

Principal: "Thanks for sharing your interest in this work. Let's have a planning meeting next Thursday at 4 p.m. We can establish conditions of satisfaction. If you're still interested, I would love for you to do it."

Teacher: "Great! I'll see you next Thursday."

At 4 p.m. on Thursday, the dance will begin.

The teacher could also make an offer: "I understand that we as a school staff are initiating a new school planning process. I was so excited to hear about this process from you at our last staff meeting. I know you said you were looking for someone to facilitate the process, and I would love to offer to do that work for you and our school.

"If you're interested, I would love to talk with you further to try to negotiate conditions of satisfaction to be sure I know what I am committing to do before I make my final promise."

A promise to fulfill the conditions of satisfaction is a commitment to meet all of the conditions of satisfaction.

Teacher: "This is exciting. I will facilitate the strategic planning process over the next nine months. I'll host regular focus groups with the staff to ensure they participate, give feedback, and engage in professional learning. I will produce written reports for the staff, you, and the superintendent about our progress."

The dance is between request and promises. The dance establishes conditions of satisfaction.

Apologies and complaints

At times, we break our promises and fail to keep commitments made as conditions of satisfaction. When that happens, the person who broke the promise apologizes immediately and re-engages in the dance to renegotiate the conditions of satisfaction. A conversation might look like this:

The first step is to apologize and repeat the commitment that is going to be broken: "I'm sorry, but I won't be able to keep my promise to have the report to you by Wednesday. I just had a major computer crash, and I have lost the document I was preparing."

The second step is to state the cost of failing to keep the promise: "I know you promised this report to the superintendent."

Next, generate a possible remedy: "I have a technician on the way. Would it be possible to renegotiate the due date? I know I can get our report to you by Thursday."

The final decision on the renegotiation is then up to the person to whom the promise was made. Moving the date may not be acceptable. A discussion of other strategies for meeting the original deadline may be needed.

When promises are broken and trust is violated, the result often is feelings of frustration and resentment. Many people believe e-mailing an apology — "Sorry I missed our meeting" — is sufficient. The person whose trust was broken may complain to others but be reluctant to speak about the matter directly with the person who broke the promise.

Making a **complaint** to someone who fails to keep a promise is an essential speech

ASSUMPTIONS

- » Language is generative.

- » Those who understand the distinctions of speech acts and practice using them are more effective at working with others.

- » Effective speech helps lead to strong, trusting relationships.

- » Communities with strong, trusting relationships effectively coordinate actions.

Keeping promises

I have a wonderful friend who also hires me to do long-term facilitation for principals in her region. We have worked together for eight years. Before and after each session, we reflect on the work we just completed. We review what we have accomplished and what steps need to be taken next. We discuss every detail. "Will you get the titles of the books we are going to use to me by next week?" "I cannot do that next week because I will not be home; will the weekend work?" "That will be fine. When will you have the slides to me? I need them by..." We discuss every detail. We make individual lists of our promises. Over years together working on this project, only a few times has either of us had to apologize for not keeping our promises. The quality of our work and the friendship and trust that have developed from negotiating conditions of satisfaction and making and keeping promises are remarkable.

act that is intended to *renew* the relationship. The steps for making a complaint are similar to those for an apology.

First, the person to whom the promise was made initiates the complaint and states the promise that was broken: "You promised to have the report on our strategic plan to me by Wednesday so that I could share it with our superintendent."

The second step is to state the damage done: "Your failure to get the report to me meant that I had to share our progress with our superintendent without your comments, and I felt totally unprepared."

The third step is to state the remedy: "I expect you to have that report to me by the end of the day tomorrow; I have scheduled another visit with the superintendent for Friday."

The person who broke the promise also may have to renegotiate an apology: "I know I failed to get you that report; I did have a computer crash late last night while I was preparing it. I realize now I should have called you first thing this morning. I apologize. I am going to have a technician help me, but he is not available until later today. Would it be possible for me to use your computer today to complete the report?"

And the dance continues.

REFLECTIONS

In conversations with others, how have you observed language to be generative?

What breakdowns have you most commonly observed in coordinating actions or work in schools?

What speech acts do you need to practice in order to engage more effectively in coordinating actions with others?

STRATEGIES AND INVESTIGATIONS

» Observe others' speech acts as they coordinate action. Make notes in your journal of what speech acts are not present and the result of those omissions. How do participants establish conditions of satisfaction? When do you notice that individuals are not establishing conditions of satisfaction? Do you observe times when declarations and requests are confused or requests are made and "begging" follows?

» When you have completed strategy one, reflect on your learning using the follow organizer.

What am I learning about myself?	
What are the personal implications of this learning?	
What are the implications for me as a coach?	
What are my next steps?	

STRATEGIES AND INVESTIGATIONS

» Recall a time when someone made you a promise and then failed to fulfill it. How did that instance show up in your language, body, and emotions?

» Remember a time when you did not keep a promise. What were the consequences? How did that show up in the body, language, and emotions of the person you made the promise to? In your own body, language, and emotions?

» Form a triad with friends or colleagues and practice negotiating conditions of satisfaction. Start small — picking up the children after school, for example — and progress to more complex issues. Ask one observer to write down any conditions of satisfaction he or she hears. Reflect on how well the negotiation generates clarity. Practice making declarations, requests, apologies, and complaints. Think about why it may be important to distinguish among them.

» Practice hosting a difficult conversation. What declarations do you need to make? To whom? What body, language, and emotions do you need to make those declarations? Is there a conversation you've been putting off because your assessment is that it will be difficult? What body, language, and emotions do you need to host that conversation? Practice with a partner. Ask for your partner's feedback.

» Consider offering to coach a friend, a superintendent, or a principal. How would you word the offer? Consider and choose the body and emotions you need in order to make this offer. If the person is interested, invite him or her to engage in the dance. Negotiate conditions of satisfaction. Whether or not you receive a commitment, reflect on your preparation and the impact that preparation had on the experience. Write your reflections in your journal.

» Help someone accomplish a goal by coaching him or her. Ask purposeful questions that would get the person to consider the body, emotions, and words essential for making a request or an offer. Ask the person to reflect on whether your coaching helped them prepare effectively for the experience. After they have made their request or offer, ask him or her to reflect with you about the experience and how preparation affected it.

RESOURCES FOR CHAPTER 8

Covey, S.M.R. (2008). *The speed of trust: The one thing that changes everything.* Indianapolis, IN: Franklin Covey.

Goman, C.K. (2011). *The silent language of leaders: How body language can help or hurt how you lead.* San Francisco: Jossey-Bass.

Lyer, S. (2011, September 23). *How to build trust in the workplace.* Available online at www.buzzle.com/articles/how-to-build-trust-in-the-workplace.html.

"Stretch goals are important because most individuals and organizations underestimate their ability to improve. Stretch goals by their very nature require important, deep changes in the organization. Achieving stretch goals requires unrelenting focus, clarity of thought, consistent communication, alignment of resources, innovation, discipline and teamwork."

— Sparks, 2007, p. 13

Coaches face the challenge of systematically helping leaders commit to new strategies that will get them different results. Yet people are challenged to work on the changes that they need to make in their own lives. Just as the nature of change varies, so do the human responses and reactions to it. Some people seem confused and confounded by change and do their best to avoid it. Others find the prospect of uncertainty invigorating, often seeking out situations that promise opportunities for new adventures and exploration. According to David Rock (2006), humans are disposed to not make change. The more experienced the brain is in certain practices, the more the brain is hardwired to repeat those actions. The solution is to create new neural firings and new pathways. Creating new pathways is the coach's role.

In a book study on Stephanie Hirsh and Joellen Killion's book, *The Learning Educator* (NSDC, 2007), the group of leaders was challenged to do only "green light thinking" — to think only in ways that would allow the idea to progress. It was nearly impossible. One participant said that people do not want to change, teachers do not want to learn, and that school districts cannot learn to focus on just a few powerful innovations. Another said, "What can we possibly do to implement these principles when others don't see the need?"

The coach's responsibility is to lead the individual being coached to green light thinking. Through questioning and envisioning, the coach helps the leader form a goal that is challenging personally and for the school. Effective coaches lead those they coach to engage in "the dance," a goal attainment process; to commit to a plan of action; to reflect on their progress; to adjust when necessary; and to celebrate their progress.

Identify the breakdown

Attaining the goal begins with identifying where a breakdown is occurring. Breakdowns interfere with individuals accomplishing their goals. One of the coach's most challenging processes is helping leaders identify what authentic breakdown they are experiencing. Getting to the heart of a hurdle requires persistent, gentle, understanding questioning. The effective coach also considers the whole person and not just the leader in his or her authority role.

Because of the coherence of the body and emotions, the individual often attaches assessments and emotions to a breakdown. Sometimes these attachments interfere with the person's thinking as well as hide the actual breakdown. For example, a person goes through two or three interviews without getting offered a new job. She attaches emotion to interviewing: "I am a failure; I am not good at interviewing. I can't get a new job." She may even go so far as to make the assessment that she will never be a principal. The coach must work diligently to explore with her, "How many jobs have you gotten? Did you interview? What other ways could you view your lack of actually getting these jobs? Were the other applicants competitive?"

Sometimes a coach might stop short of exploring real issues with the leader and never discover the authentic breakdown simply because the coach does not continue to question or to look for root causes. A breakdown may have little to do with the coached person's work. A skillful coach continues to probe and explore to uncover the authentic breakdown.

Establish a challenging, results-oriented goal

An essential coaching strategy is guiding those being coached to develop powerful goals. As Hirsh and Killion say (2007, p. 47), "Ambitious goals lead to powerful actions and remarkable results."

FIGURE 9.1 **The goal attainment process**

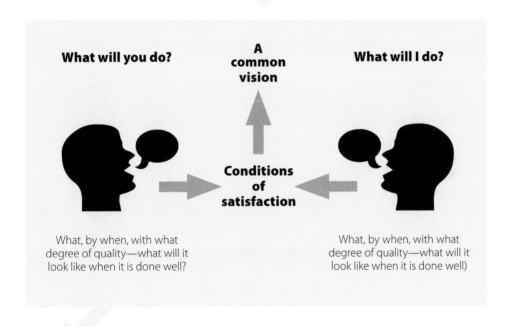

People often set a goal that is too general, such as, "I want to be healthy." Although this is a worthy goal, it is too broad to offer much direction.

Coaches help those they are coaching to develop challenging, results-oriented goals. The coach may ask them to consider what it is they really want to achieve at the end of three years, two years, one year, and next month, and why this goal is important. They might ask:

- Can you see yourself doing this?
- What are you doing?
- What will it look like when you are doing it well?
- What are you thinking?
- What does it feel like?
- Where will you do it?
- How often?
- What results will be expected?
- What barriers may get in your way?
- How are you going to overcome those barriers?

When goals are specific, leaders have the best opportunity to measure their progress. Through measuring progress, they gain confidence that they can accomplish their aim.

For example, rather than setting a goal of being healthy, the individual might be coached to articulate this goal: "I want to be physically fit. I will work out three times a week using both aerobic and weight training." These specifics give a clearer picture of what the person really would like to achieve. The individual sees the goal as specific and attainable.

One of the coach's greatest challenges is to help the leader consider realistic goals. A person whose goal is to lose 50 pounds in a month is being neither healthy nor realistic. To be realistic, a goal must represent an objective toward which the leader is willing and able to work. A goal can be both lofty and realistic; only the leader can decide how challenging the goal should be. The coach's challenge is to be sure that each goal represents substantial achievement. The individual being coached has to feel that the goal matters and should feel compelled to achieve it.

The first step to establishing a powerful, specific goal is to engage the leader in meaningful self-assessment on the essential skills of a successful principal. (See the principal self-assessment tool in Appendix A.) Through the goal-setting process, principals begin to consider the skills they need in order to lead high-achieving schools. They consider ways to ensure that their actions send a powerful message to students, staff, and parents that student learning and student well-being are at the heart of the school. They also begin to identify areas that may increase their effectiveness. For example, the leader may monitor student learning, but not chart each student's progress or talk with learning teams regularly. He or she may have lunch with students, but may not be hosting focus groups with them or the community stressing the importance of learning to children's future.

Through self-assessment, leaders begin to examine how well they engage their communities in developing a common vision for the school. They consider how to embed purposeful professional learning in teachers' workdays. They engage staff in classroom observations, action research, and protocols for examining student work. They examine their own effectiveness in focusing staff in meaningful conversations about data-driven, vision-driven curricula with common curriculum maps; instructional processes; and assessment strategies. In addition, they consider their strengths in developing leadership in students, staff, parents, and community members. Through deep, thoughtful examination of their strengths and weaknesses, they consider the area of greatest concern to them, and they explore goals that would lead them to greater proficiency.

The coach continues to focus the leader through questioning, asking:

- What have you done since last we visited to achieve your goals?
- What steps have you taken?
- What have been the results of that effort?
- What are you most proud of?
- How have you celebrated those successes?
- What challenges did you face?
- How did you overcome them?
- If you were to do this work again, what would you do differently?
- What are you learning?
- What are your next steps?

Engage in the dance

By engaging the leader in the dance, the coach guides the individual being coached to create a pathway to achieve the leader's own goal. The coach guides the leader in envisioning what accomplishing the goal will be like, asking questions such as:

- What will it look like when you have accomplished your goal?
- What will you be doing?
- What will others be doing?
- What new attitudes do you envision will emerge for you? For others?
- What new behaviors will you want to practice?
- What commitments do you need to make to others?
- What declarations?
- What requests and offers?
- What do you need to set as long-term outcomes, intermediate goals, and short-term goals?

- What plans of action are essential?
- What resources will be essential?
- What barriers might you face?
- How will you overcome those barriers?
- How will you practice essential skills often enough and long enough so they become natural to you?
- What emotions do you need to bring up to be successful?
- What body posture will you need? How will you sit? Where will your arms be?
- What will you accept as evidence that you are making progress?

Expert coaches guide leaders to avoid "should and must" thinking, which reflects a lack of energy and passion. When a leader says, "I really should call that staff meeting tomorrow to discuss this issue," the coach asks, "*Should* you out of obligation, or do you really want to call that staff meeting? Tell me about the emotions you have about this action when you use the word 'should.' "

A willing attitude is important. New skills and strategies are difficult to develop and often feel awkward and uncomfortable. Developing proficiency in using a new strategy takes hard work and practice to understand a different concept and create new neural networks to use it. After practice, though, the difficulty subsides, the task becomes easier, and we don't have to think so hard. Those new neuron maps are being hardwired. Many hours of practicing and coaching are needed before an individual can do a task well enough to stop making mistakes. A proficiency level for any new skill is at a level that the skill feels natural enough that the individual will prefer it over the old practice. To ensure this level of proficiency, the coach guides the leader to repeated, purposeful practice.

Get the commitment

The final step in the coaching-planning cycle is commitment. Planning to change is much easier than actually doing the work. A successful coach never leaves a coaching session without a commitment. The coach may ask:

- Is this really your plan of action?
- Can you really see yourself doing this?
- Are you willing to devote sufficient time to practice this skill until you are truly proficient?
- How much effort do you see yourself giving to this?
- Are there things you need to change in your plan that will help you commit more fully to make this effort?

A skillful coach never takes commitment lightly. Effective coaches spend time with those being coached to explore their level of commitment to their plans. Effective coaches reflect on their coaching at the same time: "Did I ask too many leading questions? Is this plan really the leader's plan, or did I provide too many of the ideas?

Do I sense that the leader is passionate about the work and willing to fully commit to learn this new skill or use this new strategy?" The coach has to be willing to back up and say, "I'm not sure we have a plan you are truly ready to commit to doing. What do you think? What modifications do you need to make so that you will give this your full effort, be energized by your plan, and give yourself the best opportunity to achieve it by practicing systematically?"

Engage in the practice

Recalling our definition of practice, we want to be sure that the coach expects the leader to fulfill his or her commitment to others and to engage in learning by implementing a plan well. The coach may ask the leader to practice first, either with the coach, in front of a mirror, or with others before actually attempting the strategy with the staff. Being in the practice of learning means using the strategy several times (recall Gladwell's 10,000 hours to achieve mastery) to truly learn and use it with ease.

Reflect on progress and celebrate successes

Leaders also need to be coached to establish an accountability system for their plan of action. The coach may ask:

- How will you know you are making progress?
- What will you accept as evidence you are succeeding?
- To whom do you want to be accountable?
- What strategies are you going to use to regularly reflect on your progress?
- What strategies do we want to use in our next coaching session to reflect on your progress?

Coaches are integral to ensuring leaders follow through. The coach helps the leader explore strategies to use to reflect on progress. Leaders may want to use journals to record their reflections, develop portfolios to collect artifacts and reflect on progress, or may have themselves videotaped or recorded so that they can observe their new skills and strategies and think about what they are learning. The key is to focus on strategies the leader will commit to do for systematic, purposeful reflection.

The coach then asks:

- What are you doing differently?
- What new attitudes do you have?
- What new behaviors are becoming more natural for you?
- What new energies are you experiencing?
- What are you most proud of?
- What celebrations are in order for you?
- How are you going to celebrate?
- What challenges remain?
- What stops your progress?

- What are you willing to do about your failure to proceed?
- What next steps are you willing to take?
- What shifts in our plan of action do we need to make?

An example

A principal said, "One of my greatest concerns is that I have a great vision for my school, but I have not developed commitment from most of the staff to that vision. Many staff members don't really believe that our students can succeed in school. I really want to focus on leading my school toward a shared vision and transforming teachers' thinking about students and their learning."

Listen to the coaching conversation that ensued.

IDENTIFY THE BREAKDOWN

Coach: "Talk to me a little bit more about that. What is your vision for your school and student success?"

Principal: "I see students being very successful on the state assessment, as well through habits such as resiliency, setting goals for themselves, and challenging themselves. I've said this over and over at staff meetings."

Coach: "What strategies have you used to share your vision with others? What was the result? Who *does* share the vision with you? Tell me how you have developed a shared vision."

Principal: "I've talked to them regularly about my expectations for students. They listen, smile, and then they go on teaching the same way."

Coach: "What other strategies have you used?"

Principal: "My leadership team has read several books together: *Social Intelligence*, by Daniel Goleman (Bantam Books, 2006), and Art Costa's book, *The School as a Home for the Mind* (Corwin Press, 2008). We spent time on the 21st Century Partnership website and explored a vision of skills students need. And we talked about the importance of these skills in the curriculum."

Coach: "What is the leadership team's response? How have they shown you that what they have read and learned matters to them?"

Principal: "Although they manage their teams well, I don't think they lead conversations with the teams about this vision."

Coach: "What have you done other than talk about these skills and your vision?"

Principal: "I bring it up during the staff's planning time."

Coach: "That still sounds like talking to me. What do you think? What shifts would you like to explore that might move staff into developing a deeper understanding or more intentional effort to ensure all students are mastering the standards?"

Principal: "I hadn't thought about the fact that all I do is talk about the vision. I could work with the leadership team to design model lesson plans that would reflect when students are proficient in the habits essential to their success."

Coach: "If you were helping the leadership team design model lesson plans, what would the process look like for you? What would the result be? Does doing this work with the leadership team really matter to you? To your students' success? How would you start the process? Who else would you involve?"

ESTABLISH THE GOAL

The coach continued: "Do you think you're ready to craft a thoughtful, focused, measurable, challenging goal for yourself? Let's try."

Principal: "By the end of the school year, I want every grade level and course team to embed the 21st-century skills and habits of the mind intentionally into every unit of study so that students develop competencies in the skills and attitudes that matter most to them in the long run."

Coach: "Let's talk about that goal. Is it strategic and focused? Can you envision this really happening by the end of the school year?"

Principal: "Yes. I can facilitate the team meetings and model for the leadership team how to design integrated units of study during their regularly scheduled collaboration time."

Coach: "What evidence will you accept that teams are effectively teaching these skills to students?"

Principal: "I can plan to have teams share their units at the monthly staff meetings. I'll also plan to visit classrooms regularly to determine how effective the new instructional design really is. I know we may get just mechanical implementation at first, but I am confident that after a few units, this work will become more meaningful to students and staff. I think we will also need to begin looking at assessments that measure these skills. I'm sure we will want to add more performance tasks and reflective practices for students."

ENGAGE IN THE DANCE

Coach: "I'm beginning to envision your goal becoming a reality. Let's design a plan of action to ensure it happens. What is your vision? What will the staff be doing? What will students be doing? What will you be doing? What will you see when you visit classrooms? What will you hear? What will the outcomes be? What long-term, intermediate, and short-term goals do you need to set for yourself? What timelines are you going to establish? What resources will you need? What barriers will you face? How will you overcome them? Who will you turn to for assistance? When and how often will you measure your progress? What artifacts will you collect to reflect your efforts and your learning?"

Identify the breakdown

I was working with a group of principals who were physically and emotionally worn down by their work. I began asking them what energized them, how they relaxed, what they did for fun. Knowing that leaders work long hours, I expected the responses I got.

"I don't have time for myself!"

"I can't remember the last time I took a walk."

"I used to play basketball with my friends every weekend; I haven't been able to do that this year."

One young principal had just been hospitalized for a week for unexplained severe abdominal pain. I asked her if I could coach her. We set to work identifying the breakdown that was showing up for her emotionally and physically.

I began questioning her: "What do you love about your work?"

She responded thoughtfully, "Facilitating my staff to do things they don't think they can do. But we have so many required things now, we hardly think about our goals."

"Under what conditions could you get more control?" I asked.

She had little to say. We explored strategies for getting a clearer focus in her school and how she might feel powerful enough to lead the school out of activity-based, haphazard, frantic behavior. After several focused questions, she had a positive goal and plan of action.

I asked, "Are you willing to really commit to do these things?"

"I can't wait to meet with my staff and explore these ideas with them," she answered. Her shoulders were lifted, and she had more color in her skin.

I continued, "What do you love to do? What gives you energy in your personal life? What excites you? What takes you away from the world because you are totally immersed in this activity?"

Without hesitation, she responded,

"I'm a musician. I taught music. I love to play the piano and used to play for hours. I haven't had time to play for years."

"Do you have a piano at home?" I asked.

"Of course!" she answered. "But I never touch it. I have so much to do here and a young child. I have housework and cooking. I don't have time to play, but I do really miss it!"

"Let's look at a calendar. Would you be willing to figure out a time to play?" I continued.

"Of course, but … " she said, hesitating.

"Would you be willing to consider the possibility you could get back to the thing you love and that gives you energy?" I asked.

"Absolutely!" she said.

"Let's consider what it would look like for you," I continued. "How much time do you really want to play? How often? What would you be willing to give up? When is the best time of day for you to play? I am going to give you some quiet time to look at your schedule, think about your day, and consider the possibility that you could spend time regularly doing what you really love."

After a period of quiet reflection, the young woman looked up.

"I know exactly where the time is for me!" she said. "I come home exhausted; I get a drink, and I watch the news. It's depressing for me, but I do it every day. I am going to use that 30 minutes every weekday to play."

"Are you going to commit to this new practice?" I asked. "Are you really willing to do this for yourself?"

"I'm excited!" she said.

"Will you do this for 30 days until you have this new practice as part of your daily routine?" I asked her. "Are you willing to start tonight?"

I did not see this principal the next day, but she called me. "I played the piano last night just as I committed to do. I feel so excited and renewed. Thanks!"

I reminded her of her 30-day commitment, and asked her again whether she was determined to engage in her new practice long enough to make it a habit. She said she was. She was re-energized. She did not feel the pain in her stomach for the first day in a long time.

GET A COMMITMENT

Coach: "You've developed a very strategic, focused, powerful goal and plan of action. Tell me about your commitment. Are you going to follow through? Does the thought of achieving your goal energize you? Motivate you?"

Principal: "Well, I'm nervous but excited. I really can see myself doing this!"

Coach: "But are you going to do it?"

Principal: "I want to do it. I have a dream for my school, and I haven't been leading the staff, students, and parents to share my vision for their future success."

Coach: "The fact that you want to do it is not really a commitment, either. What commitment are you really making? What will your first steps be? When will you take them? Will you be willing to do these things before we visit again? Will you commit to sharing the outcomes of your work and bringing artifacts that reflect your progress?"

Principal: "Yes! I'll take the first steps I designed, and when you see me next, I will have artifacts to share."

Commitment!

Another story

Another principal had little energy for the work she and the coach were doing in the coaching session. She and the coach were developing strategies for embedding professional learning into teachers' days. She had shared over several sessions how staff members were not engaged. They did their jobs, but they seemed just to be coming to work and going home as soon as they could. She felt challenged to get them focused on data and building meaningful relationships with students, and to helping them commit to increasing student success. Here is how the conversation went.

IDENTIFY THE BREAKDOWN

Coach: "What evidence do you have that teachers are not connecting with their students?"

Principal: "They show no interest when we talk about student performance on standardized tests. They sit quietly and barely answer my questions when I visit with the teams."

Coach: "What do you think is contributing to this sense of apathy?"

Principal: "I think they're exhausted. We initiated several new things this year, changes not based on our plans but directed by the district. We have a new reading series, a new math series, and a new approach to teaching writing all at the same time. We have new primary assessments that must be done on PalmPilots. We have a new schedule, new expectations for professional learning from the district, and we just received the data from our balanced scorecard. I have to bring this data to the staff tomorrow. I know how they're going to respond, and I don't want to spend time on it, but the district says I have to."

Coach: "Let's examine this. Who is exhausted?"

Principal: "Honestly, I am exhausted. I spent a month in the hospital this fall with an embolism. My 21-year-old daughter was just released from the hospital after she survived a life-threatening disease, and I put my mother in a nursing home last week. I could not take care of her anymore, but I feel so guilty about not being there for her when she needs me so much."

Coach: "How do you think the way you are feeling right now impacts your staff?"

Principal: "Maybe my feelings are generating the exhaustion in them. Maybe I'm not seeing them as they are. They are really good teachers."

Coach: "What other observations could you make about the staff?"

Principal: "Maybe they're tired of all the new efforts because I'm tired of the mandates. I feel I have no control over this school's direction. I used to think I was a good principal."

Coach: "What evidence do you have right now that you are not in control? That you are not a good principal? What assessments are you making that are and are not grounded?"

Principal: "We have accomplished a lot this year. We have a new one-on-one tutoring program that the teachers implemented as part of our school plan. We designed it based on our research, and teachers are excited about the results of that work on student learning."

Coach: "What else have you done that you are excited about?"

Principal: "We initiated two parent nights this year, one for literacy and one for math. A lot of parents attended. Kids loved it. Teachers were so encouraged, they plan two more this winter."

Coach: "What else have you accomplished as a staff this year?"

As the conversation continued, color seeped back into the principal's face. Her body became more upright. The coach could see pride reflected in her tone and language, and the pace of the conversation increased. She looked neither tired nor dejected.

Coach: "I think I am hearing that you accomplished many things you set out to accomplish this year. Is that correct?"

Principal: "Yes. It's really rather amazing. I haven't thought back to all the work we have done."

Coach: "And you and your staff planned to do those things. They were not mandated. Is that correct?"

Principal: "Yes."

Coach: "Would you be willing to list all your and the staff's accomplishments this year?"

Principal: "That would be fun!"

Coach: "Why don't you do it now?" The two paused.

ASSUMPTIONS

» As coach and leader engage in conversations about goals and clearly articulate them, the leader has the best opportunity to achieve them.

» Challenging goals without a clearly articulated plan of action lead to frustration.

The coach continued: "Am I hearing that on top of all your goals and the work that you did, you really all are tired because of all the stress of doing what you set out to do and implementing with fidelity what the district wants you to. Is that correct?"

Principal: "Absolutely!"

Coach: "Have you done what the district expects?"

Principal: "We're learning. We're not doing them all well. They're too big."

Coach: "Is it true this is all new learning for you?"

Principal: "No, teachers in this building have been teaching reading well. We're just trying to learn the new series."

Coach: "Are you finding much resistance?"

Principal: "Some, but it's really minimal, and mainly teachers are problem solving."

Coach: "So those strategies are going well even though they are new and teachers are facing new learning around them. Am I hearing you correctly? I don't want to put words in your mouth. I just want to clarify what I am hearing."

Principal: "Really, I think they are going quite well."

ESTABLISH THE GOAL

Coach: "If you believe that's true, what outcome might you want after tomorrow's meeting that would renew the energy in the school both for you and for the staff?"

Principal: "I think we need a celebration! I used to be fun. I used to come dressed up and let staff enjoy our time together. We've forgotten to have fun along the way. We have a lot to celebrate, and I haven't even thought about it. I've just been anxious and pushing to get the next thing done. No wonder we've all been sick and exhausted."

ENGAGE IN THE DANCE

Coach: "Do you want to explore other strategies you would be willing to do tomorrow other than going over the balanced score card, strategies that will renew your energy?"

With renewed enthusiasm and passion, the school leader committed to her plan of action.

Coach: "OK. Let's explore what the celebration will look like. Will it occur during the 45 minutes we have allocated to the score card?"

Principal: "We could use the success analysis protocol and have each team generate their greatest accomplishments — the things they are most proud of."

Coach: "That sounds like fun. Do you think the staff will enjoy it?"

Principal: "They'll love it. They love to talk about what they do well. We can also ask people to thank their teammates for their contributions to the team."

She had more ideas.

Principal: "I have some gratitude cards. People can write notes to each other during the session, stand up and thank people publicly, and give them a card. We can have gifts and door prizes. I have lots of bookmarks I have been trying to figure out how to use. They will each get one. I'll dress up and come to the celebration dancing to the music, 'Celebrate Good Times.' "

Coach: "Now you're in the spirit."

Principal: "We can have make-your-own ice cream sundaes, and I'll get a variety of ice cream, including diet food. I better get to the store!"

She laughed. "My staff will be shocked! We have only been pushing forward; tomorrow, I'm going to make sure everyone is celebrated."

The coach asked her to email the agenda and call after the celebration. The principal promised to do so.

REFLECTIONS

What did you learn about establishing powerful goals, engaging in the dance, establishing a plan of action to change behavior, getting commitments to action and practice, and reflecting on learning?

What seems natural to you?

What challenges you?

What new strategies do you have?

What do you want to learn next?

STRATEGIES AND INVESTIGATIONS

» In the face of Hitler's expanding reach in World War II, Winston Churchill declared that England would do whatever it took to protect itself:

"Even though large tracts of Europe and many old and famous states have fallen or may fall into the grip of the Gestapo and all the odious apparatus of Nazi rule, we shall not flag or fail. We shall go on to the end. We shall fight in France, we shall fight on the seas and oceans, we shall fight with growing confidence and growing strength in the air, we shall defend our island, whatever the cost may be. We shall fight on the beaches, we shall fight on the landing grounds, we shall fight in the fields and in the streets, we shall fight in the hills; we shall never surrender, and if, which I do not for a moment believe, this island or a large part of it were subjugated and starving, then our Empire beyond the seas, armed and guarded by the British Fleet, would carry on the struggle, until, in God's good time, the new world, with all its power and might, steps forth to the rescue and the liberation of the old" (Churchill, 1940).

Churchill issued a clear, challenging goal for a nation facing huge odds. Think of some challenging goals the United States has faced. How did the goals facilitate the nation's success? What can we learn about facilitating goal setting to develop an understanding of how others have achieved the impossible?

» Think of goals that you have achieved. How and why were you inspired to achieve them? What did they look like? Were they audacious, challenging, results-oriented goals?

» Consider those you are coaching. What questions and strategies will you use to help them establish, refine, and/or clarify their goals to become challenging, results-oriented goals? What protocols do you need to establish to be sure you are asking questions that would guide them to establishing challenging, results-oriented goals? Develop those in your coach's portfolio or journal.

» Practice developing challenging, results-oriented goals for yourself. Ask a partner coach to examine your goals and to help you make sure they are specific, measurable, attainable, results-oriented, and time-bound.

» Develop strategies to engage leaders in the dance. What questions will you be sure to ask? What questions will allow leaders to design their own plan? Record your thinking, reflections, and powerful questions in your journal.

STRATEGIES AND INVESTIGATIONS

» Ask a principal or a friend to allow you to practice your new skills with them to ensure that they establish clearly articulated, challenging, results-oriented goals and develop a strategic plan of action. Be sure to complete the dance with full commitment to action, strategies for sufficient embedded practice, and strategies for reflections, celebrations, and redirection to ensure the goal is achieved. Debrief with this person as to what was effective about your coaching session and what was not as easy or clear. Make notes in your journal about what you learned from the session.

» Ask a friend if you may practice your skills or ask if he or she is willing to implement the plan and to have a follow-up session with you about the outcomes. Plan carefully for the follow-up session to ensure the person coached had opportunities to reflect on his or her work, practice, successes, and challenges. Engage your friend in next-step thinking.

» Practice helping leaders by using the process yourself: Set your own challenging, results-oriented goal, commit to your own action plan, and reflect on your learning. Coach yourself to strengthen these skills in your own learning.

» Videotape or audiotape several coaching sessions over time. Reflect on what you are learning. What new skills are emerging for you? What is beginning to feel natural to you? What skills are you using with precision? What differences do you see in those you coach as you develop your skill? What are you most proud of in your learning? What do you need to celebrate? What do you need to modify in your plan of action? What next steps will you commit to?

» Ask a fellow coach to observe several videos or listen to several audiotapes of your coaching sessions. Ask the coach to explore his or her observations with you. Generate new and creative ways to strengthen your coaching skills.

RESOURCES FOR CHAPTER 9

Goleman, D., Boyatzis, R., & McKee, A. (2002). *Primal leadership: Realizing the power of emotional intelligence.* Boston: Harvard Business School Press.

Underhill, B.O., McAnally, K., Koriath, J.J., & Leider, R.J. (2007). *Executive coaching for results: The definitive guide to developing organizational leaders.* New York: Berrett-Koehler Publishers.

"Learning does not mean acquiring more information, but expanding the ability to produce the results we truly want in life. It is lifelong generative learning. And learning organizations are not possible unless they have people at every level who practice."

— *Senge, 1994, p. 142*

T wo Chinese characters are needed to form the word "learning," according to Peter Senge (1994). He writes that the first Chinese character is a symbol that means "to study," placed above a symbol for a child in a doorway, leading to the meaning "to accumulate knowledge." A second character, a bird leaving a nest, means "to practice constantly." Together these two suggest that learning is continuous practice such that we become proficient. This explanation is the essence of what is required of both the coach and the leader: study and constant practice leading to self-improvement.

Transforming schools and coaching school leadership teams requires an understanding of how schools learn and change. Highly effective school coaches understand curriculum, instruction, and assessment design and can help principals

The Chinese characters for "learning."

become instructional leaders. They are grounded in the principles and practices of professional learning.

The effective coach also understands systems thinking in light of data-driven decision making; effective collaboration; systems of curriculum, instruction, and assessment; teacher leadership; student discipline; and parent and community involvement. Principals work with multiple, complex, even competing systems that are interdependent. School leaders need to be helped to understand the concept of learning to learn in order to understand change and its effects at a systems level.

Coaches understand that learning occurs when there is a gap between what we want (our vision) and where we are. This gap causes those in the organization to work with each other, to develop strong relationships, to search for new approaches and to learn to achieve their vision. To fill that gap, coaches learn strategies to help principals design systems for building shared vision and for developing logic models grounded in thoughtful theories.

Coaches who are most effective in helping principals build high-achieving schools ground themselves in the concepts or principles as well as the research about learning communities and increased student success. For schools to achieve their goals, they must be learning organizations.

Learning organizations

Senge (1994) has written extensively on the nature of systems, systems theory, and systems thinking. Because systems are interdependent in organizations, any shift in one system impacts all other systems. Those who lead schools must be systems thinkers so that they can make decisions that consider all the possible shifts that may be experienced in the system. An organization is made up of many administrative and management functions, products, services, groups, and individuals. If one part of the system is changed, the nature of the overall system often changes. Those who work in schools are engaged in complex systems work, and those who coach schools and leaders need a deep understanding of the nature of systems and systems change.

Principals of successful schools design an environment and create conditions that allow all in the school to move from *change fragile* to *change agile*. Jayme Rolls, a psychologist and president of a consulting firm focusing on transformational leadership, says, "Change is the constant. The only way to survive is as a learning organization — one that can continuously adapt, learn, be change-responsive, to reinvent the reality and the future, to transform" (1995, p. 102).

Highly effective principals are growth-oriented and willing to live in ambiguity. They take risks that are likely to result in improved student and staff learning. They value creativity, in themselves and in others. They are on a personal journey to become moral architects, coaches, stewards, relationship builders, and models for others of authenticity, courage, and commitment.

Effective systems coaches inspire those they coach to become model learners. When principals work toward personal mastery, they develop a shared vision and are able to articulate what is needed to move toward that vision. When all individuals in the organization are learning and growing together, shifts happen.

Kofman and Senge (1995, p. 32) state that a learning organization is grounded in:

- A culture based on transcendent human values of love, wonder, humility, and compassion;
- A set of practices for generative conversation and coordinated action; and
- A capacity "to see and work with the flow of life as a system."

Practices that lead to generative conversations and coordinated action in learning schools include using data to understand student needs, collaboratively designing curriculum and instruction, and regularly monitoring student progress. Through these efforts, according to Hord and Sommers (2008), learning teams begin to develop a shared vision, values and goals, effective collaborative processes, effective strategies for planning and celebrating successes, systematic processes for engaging the community in learning, and strategies for distributing leadership throughout the school.

Data, disequilibrium, and vision building

One strategy for systems change is building disequilibrium in the organization through using data, shared vision, and feedback loops. Effective coaches help the principal keep the organization living and learning — slightly off balance. Equilibrium is the death knell of organizations. When those within the organization are not drawn to a new vision or to change, complacency threatens the organization's very existence. Many educators today believe that student achievement is outside their control and other factors are the cause of poor performance — parents not doing homework with students, disengaged students, students who don't care about school. Others shift responsibility to the administration, saying, "We're doing what the district tells us to. Student performance is their responsibility." Some schools and districts with high-achieving students have the attitude, "We're better than most. So let's not do anything differently or learn anything new in case it affects our test scores." When teachers own the data and have the sense that they can produce different results, they are inspired to learn and implement innovations.

Principals who focus on student outcomes develop powerful systems around data. They ensure that assessments of student learning are appropriately rigorous and aligned with state standards in order to give teams reliable information about student progress. They create systems to monitor every child's progress, both for themselves and for their teaching teams, balancing statistical data with examination of student work. They host frequent, meaningful conversations with staff about student performance data. Data conversations result in the principal and teaching teams taking new actions. A valued coach has a deep understanding of these elements and can help the school leader design, implement, and modify these systems when they break down.

Shared vision

The strategies that facilitate this need to learn and change are the school's clear understanding of its current condition and the distance between that condition and the staff's dreams and aspirations for the school. Schools need assistance in developing a clearly articulated, shared vision around any change effort using that vision to measure progress.

School leaders may use a variety of strategies to develop shared vision. Some use a school leadership team to facilitate staff conversations. They read about and research what highly effective schools look like. They study schools that have developed powerful learning communities for students and staff. They clarify what their school will look like over time.

Some schools may develop a vision over time. They may start with a particular aspect of the school, such as the relationships between students and staff or a desire for a more powerful curriculum.

In Killeen, Texas, Iduma Elementary opened primarily to serve students whose parents were stationed at Fort Hood just as the U.S. began war with Iraq. During challenging times, staff members decided to establish a vision to guide their decision making (see Figure 10.1).

With coaching, the leadership team created a clearly articulated vision statement. They then began the process of determining what that vision really looked like to them: What will students be doing? Staff? What will the curriculum look like? What assessment strategies will be essential? What instructional practices will matter the most? How will we know we are making progress? How will we evaluate our progress?

Iduma school staff regularly celebrated opportunities to serve the children of the community and continuously learned new ways to ensure the highest-quality curriculum for all. Their work was nested in a culture of meaningful relationships.

FIGURE 10.1 Iduma Elementary School vision

Our vision of our school

Iduma Elementary School
Killeen (Texas) Intermediate School District

Everyone in the school community is energized by and passionate about achieving our mission. We have a deep understanding of the challenges facing our school community, and everyone contributes continuously.

Our vision:

We are a fun-loving, collaborative, focused, enthusiastic, risk-taking, intelligent community of learners with a reputation for excellence.

When we are achieving our vision, we will observe the following in our school:

Students engage in learning what is meaningful to them and make significant progress in achieving state and national standards. They value learning; they respect themselves and others; they share in the responsibility of a democratic school in which all achieve at high levels.

Staff members engage in continuous learning. We use research and data to guide our decisions. We support each other and mentor each other so that all are highly competent. We share the responsibility for all students in the school and acknowledge our power and control to change those aspects of the school that have the greatest impact on student learning. We meaningfully engage students, parents, and community members in understanding the learning process, the expectations for student success, and ways they can powerfully partner with us.

Parents and community members engage as equal partners in ensuring the success of all students. They make positive contributions at school, in their businesses and places of community service, and at home to ensure students are healthy and engaged in learning.

Source: Killeen Independent School District.

Schools are learning communities when every teacher is learning every day the strategies and processes that best meet the needs of every child in the school.

As a school community, staff members continuously worked to make their vision a reality. They routinely asked, "What will our relationships be like when our school is highly effective in meeting the needs of all students? What will we see in the school? What will children be doing, saying, feeling?"

Vision work is daily work, and an effective coach is continuously working with the principal and the school leadership team to develop systems that sustain these efforts.

Principles of professional learning

Effective coaches of principals ground themselves in the principles and standards of professional learning. When coaches are unaware of the essential characteristics of professional learning, principals may be at a loss as to what strategies are most effective for teachers to learn together. School-based coaches understand these standards so well that they are constantly guiding schools to understand them and use them to move the school forward. Coaches help schools use the standards to develop annual professional development plans, to embed professional learning into every staff member's daily life, and to determine the strategies they need to develop in the school for all to learn well. (See Appendix D: Learning Forward's Standards for Professional Learning.)

Schools are learning communities when every teacher is learning every day the strategies and processes that best meet the needs of every child in the school. Many people still have a vision of staff development occurring outside of school. They do not see the power or value of daily, embedded professional learning. Embedded professional learning is a natural part of the school day. Teachers observe each other, design lessons together, conduct action research or walk-throughs, and use these strategies regularly to change their teaching practices. Powerful professional learning is results-oriented; it changes teacher behaviors in such a way that student learning increases.

Effective coaches are so grounded in these concepts, principles, and strategies of professional learning that they can help principals build professional learning communities where all students achieve at a high level.

The coach is skilled in helping those being coached develop strategies and proto-cols to lead staff members to learn well.

Challenging, results-oriented goals

Once the vision is clearly articulated and grounded in reliable, valid research about student and adult learning, the school coach engages the leadership team in using student performance data and what is known about the school to establish challenging, results-oriented goals for the school. Goals stretch and challenge the organization to accelerate its efforts to achieve its vision. Even when the vision is compelling, achieving it can seem overwhelming. When schools establish challenging, results-oriented goals, they can measure their progress along the way to achieving their vision, celebrate their progress, and grow more confident that they can achieve whatever they set out to achieve. The school coach is instrumental in assisting and leading teams in challenging themselves and establishing rigor in their work.

Theory of change and logic models

Once the principal and leadership team clearly articulate their vision and establish their goals, they turn their attention to clarifying their theory of how to achieve the vision and goals. The coach helps the leadership team develop a stated theory of change. This is important because all organizations are led by explicit or unstated theories of how change occurs.

A research-based theory of change:

- Helps a principal become more strategic about ways to implement plans;
- Allows a principal to build a change strategy that is consistent with best practices in developing professional learning communities;
- Makes the change process explicit so that people can talk about it; and
- Gets at the organization's culture and creates a potential for transformation.

A sound theory of change considers a system for developing shared vision around a new innovation, clearly articulated plans of action, strategies for community learning and work, and evaluation systems. As principals and other leaders in the school begin to describe in a transparent way how the organization can move from its current condition to its desired outcome, the coach helps the leadership team begin to define the essential steps and possible breakdowns that may thwart movement toward the vision and goals.

What is a theory of change? A theory of change is a process of backward mapping to ensure the desired outcomes. Those who develop the theory of change describe cause-and-effect relationships and mental models of how change occurs in the organization. They discuss those elements inherent in the organization's structures and systems that are not usually obvious to those in the organization, elements that both

FIGURE 10.2 A theory of change

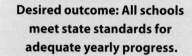

Desired outcome: All schools meet state standards for adequate yearly progress.

All schools develop a shared vision around professional learning and the impact of their learning on student learning.

Principals visit with each team of teachers to help teams achieve their goals.

All grade-level and content-area teams analyze student performance data to determine students' greatest needs and set challenging, results-oriented goals for themselves.

All teaching teams monitor each student's performance and analyze their data as a community every three weeks to design the next three weeks of instruction, to group and regroup students, and to extend learning opportunities for students who have not been successful.

All teams develop common curriculum maps, common assessments of and for learning, and common instructional plans to address the standards and immerse students in the skills essential for them to succeed.

facilitate goal attainment and prevent it. The design of the theory of change creates a sense of relationships that will allow the staff to achieve its goal.

Some schools' theory of change is quite simple: Leaders tell staff what to do, and staff members do it.

This theory, which is often the operational theory for schools, does not build commitment. Those in the organization become complacent, wait to be told what to do, and blame the "teller" when things do not go well.

In complex organizations like schools, structures and pathways for change are far more challenging. When principals know how to work with others to develop a theory of change, they engage others in creating a map to achieve success. Debates may generate strategies for continuous learning, overcoming barriers, and for redirecting when strategies are not working. Whether the principal can lead in new ways, see things he or she has never seen before, and implement innovations may depend on a coach's skill in guiding a team to build a thoughtful, successful theory of how change will occur in the organization.

FIGURE 10.3 **Logic model**

Goal	Long-term outcomes	Intermediate goals	Short-term goals	Outputs		Resources
Challenging, results-oriented goal and rationale.	Changes in culture.	Change in skill.	Change in understanding.	What we do.	Who we reach.	What we need.
Data, need.	Knowledge, attitudes, skills, proficiency, aspirations.	Behavior, practices, policies, procedures.	Awareness, motivation, understanding.	Coaching, facilitation, modeling.	Teachers. principals, support staff.	Time, money, books, substitutes.

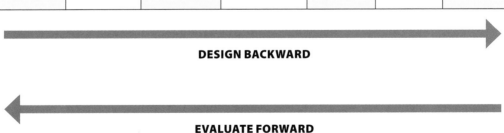

DESIGN BACKWARD

EVALUATE FORWARD

FIGURE 10.4 Stafford County (Va.) school planning theory of change and logic model

Theory of change

Intended results/goal: All schools are professional learning communities.

School staff members establish a clear vision for their school grounded in meaningful beliefs about student and adult learners.

School staff members establish school priorities and plans based on student needs, current research and thinking in the field, external factors that impact the school, and data about student performance.

School staff members align individual teachers' professional development goals with school and district goals to increase student achievement.

Logic model

Inputs/resources	Activities/processes	Intermediate outcomes
Principals, central office administrators, and school leadership team members are trained in processes for powerful planning.	Office of professional development contracts with consultant to provide training.	Principals, working with their leadership teams, develop a clear vision for their school grounded in beliefs about students and adult learners.
Lead teachers are trained in standards, assessments, and data-driven decision making.	Supervisors and coordinators develop the leadership capacity of lead teachers.	Schools establish priorities based on the needs of students, current research and thinking in the field, external factors that impact the school, and data about student performance.
Lead teachers are trained in coaching and other forms of job-embedded staff development.	The office of professional development provides training in assessment and classroom walk-throughs.	Professional development is evaluated in terms of student outcomes.

FIGURE 10.4 Stafford County (Va.) school planning theory of change and logic model

Theory of change

Goal:

Rationale (research to support the goal):

Assumptions:

Long-term outcomes	Intermediate goals	Short-term goals	Outputs	Resources

FIGURE 10.4 Stafford County (Va.) school planning theory of change and logic model

Example

Goal:
All students increase problem-solving strategies and mathematical reasoning skills as reflected in quarterly districtwide benchmark assessments by 20% each quarter.

Rationale (research to support the goal):
As students increase their skills in mathematical reasoning and problem solving, they become more effectively skilled to meet the challenges not only in our curriculum, but in the world around them (Resnick, n.d.).

Assumptions:

- Teachers who design common instructional systems capitalize on the creativity of everyone on the team.
- Teaching teams who design common assessments for learning assist students by giving them immediate feedback on their learning.
- Monitoring student learning quarterly assists teaching teams in monitoring student progress, informing their instructional practices, and differentiating effectively to meet student needs.

Intended results:
June 2006: School improvement plans follow a consistent format grounded in research and focused on professional learning communities.

June 2007: Teachers work in professional learning communities to review ongoing student performance and to identify personal learning goals.

June 2008: Teachers participate in site-based professional development aligned with school and district goals.

June 2009: Schools evaluate the effectiveness of their SIP and Professional Development plans in terms of student outcomes.

FIGURE 10.4 Stafford County (Va.) school planning theory of change and logic model

Example

Long-term outcomes	Intermediate goals	Short-term goals	Outputs	Resources
Due to their conceptual understanding of mathematics, students are more effective problem solvers.	Establish common assessments to monitor student progress. Establish a system to effectively monitor student learning. Implement a system for differentiating instruction based on data. Design and implement a process for teachers to observe each other teach. Host quarterly meetings with the principal to discuss strategies for meeting the needs of each child.	Establish common formats among grade levels for planning lessons to strengthen problem solving and mathematical reasoning. Establish system for designing and teaching anchor lessons. Identify anchor work of students to reflect high-quality mathematical reasoning and problem solving.	Common assessments for learning among all grade levels. Data charts reflecting student growth in mathematical reasoning and problem solving. Anchor lessons of teachers that produce high-quality work in students. Anchor work to assist teaching teams in determining quality work from students.	Common planning time. Books for a book study on effectively teaching mathematical reasoning and problem solving.

The coach then guides the principal to build purposeful logic models based on a thoughtful theory of change. Logic models began to emerge in the 1970s as organizations clarified their thinking about how best to achieve their goals. Logic models also facilitate evaluation. A logic model breaks down the components of the theory of change into checkpoints. Logics models are protocols for designing backward (see Figure 10.3). The coach guides principals to begin with the end in mind and clarify the goals they expect to achieve. Through thoughtful dialogue and conversation, the principal uses backward design to chart a path to success.

As coaches help principals establish logic models, principals grow in understanding organizational change and make more strategic decisions that accelerate learning and success.

For example, in Stafford County, Va., Director of Professional Development Pat Wiedel established the following theory of change and logic model before beginning a major restructuring initiative (see Figure 10.4).

Effective coaches help the school leader and staff work together to develop logic models that align with their theory of change and ensure purposeful movement toward successful implementation of the innovation.

Innovation Configurations

A skilled coach can help the principal and leadership team develop an Innovation Configuration that teachers can use to determine how well they are achieving the desired change. An Innovation Configuration is an effective, researched approach to identifying and describing major components of the new practice and the continuum of progress observers might see as those involved in the innovation move toward high-quality implementation (see Figure 10.5).

Teachers might begin implementation by sharing their thinking. As they work with others and engage in more powerful implementation to achieve the desired outcome, their modeling out loud develops into greater precision in their practice. Teams that work to develop an Innovation Configuration begin to declare what the innovation really looks like, from its beginning stages to fidelity.

Essentials for change

Another powerful tool in the coach's tool kit is a KASAB chart. A KASAB chart defines the changes in knowledge, attitudes, skills, aspirations, and behaviors that result from professional learning focused on challenging, results-oriented goals or strategies from the school's plan. A KASAB chart helps teams define and establish essential behaviors, dispositions, and knowledge required for changes to be effective for students and staff. In addition, a KASAB chart (see Figure 10.6) is a valuable tool in evaluating how well the team achieved its goals and where breakdowns may have occurred.

FIGURE 10.5 Example of an Innovation Configuration

Desired outcome I: Teachers verbalize their mathematical reasoning for students.

Level 1	Level 2	Level 3	Level 4	Level 5
The teacher verbalizes all of his or her mathematical thinking prior to solving the problem. The teacher clearly articulates several possible strategies to use, how to attack the problem, strategies for identifying what is important in the problem, and the way he or she plans to solve it. The teacher verbalizes clearly what is confusing to him or her about the problem and the challenges that are posed in solving it.	The teacher verbalizes his or her mathematical thinking prior to solving the problem. The teacher articulates a strategy about how to attack the problem and a possible plan of action to solve the problem. The teacher identifies strategies for determining what is important in the problem and ways he or she might solve the problem effectively.	The teacher verbalizes some mathematical thinking prior to solving the problem. The teacher articulates a strategy for solving the problem but does not elaborate on a plan of action prior to solving the problem. The teacher spends little time looking at alternatives or determining importance in different ways to approach the problem. The teacher does not model or express out loud his or her confusion about a problem so that students see the challenges in the problem.	The teacher focuses on solving the problem and does not verbalize his or her mathematical thinking.	

> ### ASSUMPTIONS
>
> » Learning is an ongoing, continuous process if we are to improve, both personally and professionally.
>
> » Schools are living systems. Change in one part affects other parts. Therefore, leaders and coaches need to understand systems thinking before working to create change.
>
> » The gap between what exists and a vision of what could be — disequilibrium — is the greatest motivator.
>
> » Coaches and leaders have specific tools and strategies that they can use to help lead staffs to create higher-achieving schools.

How does a team develop a KASAB chart? First, learners agree they see a clear and compelling need for change and are ready to implement an innovation called for in the school plan. Teams of teachers and administrators, parents, and students may work together to develop the KASAB. Some participants may have been on action teams or research teams that determined which innovation the school will try and may have researched and worked on establishing a theory of change. A skilled coach guides the leadership team to help participants clarify the types of change and behavior required.

Effective coaches of principals and school leadership teams have skills in systems thinking and understand change. They coach principals in developing effective systems and strategies that lead schools to higher achievement. Schools that need a coach often have experienced years of failure, and staff may have developed resentment and/or resignation. The coach needs wisdom, skills, and confidence that coaching will result in renewed learning, energy, and student and staff success.

FIGURE 10.6 Example of a KASAB chart
Implementation of new science course of study

Changes in knowledge, attitude, skill, aspiration, and behavior that will result from professional development.			
Types of change	**Teachers**	**Principals**	**Central office**
KNOWLEDGE Conceptual understanding of information, theories, principles, and research.	Teachers understand the science content standards and the Understanding by Design (UbD) framework as it connects to quality work in science.	Principals understand what they will look for and see in classroom science instruction and gain knowledge of curricular changes and shifts.	Administrators make connections between science curriculum and the district campus improvement plan goals for curriculum and professional development goals.
ATTITUDE Beliefs about the value of particular information or strategies.	Teachers believe in the importance of "understanding" rather than "coverage" in instruction, assessment, and real-life applications of science.	Principals believe in and value the backward design framework and support its use through building-level professional development.	The central office values teacher collaboration in science planning and responds to individual team needs.
SKILL Strategies or processes to apply knowledge.	Teachers employ UbD strategies to help students demonstrate deep understanding of key concepts in science.	Principals identify characteristics of quality instruction by teachers and quality work by students in science by demonstrating understanding.	Central office administrators continuously build their repertoire of skills related to UbD that enables them to meet professional learning needs in science instruction.
ASPIRATION Desire and internal motivation to engage in a particular practice.	Teachers espouse a genuine desire for their students to perform well in science on tests and authentic performance tasks.	Principals embrace the need to include UbD and science knowledge in order to foster teacher growth.	The central office provides differentiated levels of professional learning to support teachers in implementing science.
BEHAVIOR Consistent application of knowledge and skills.	Teachers consistently evidence use of UbD practices and performance tasks in science to help students acquire deep understanding of key concepts.	Principals partner with the central office to support teacher development of UbD and new science practices on an ongoing basis.	The central office provides a consistent vehicle for sharing quality science work and strategies.

REFLECTIONS

What big ideas stand out for you about change, organizational learning, and the value of coaching?

What new actions and strategies are open to you?

What new skills are you developing as a coach?

STRATEGIES AND INVESTIGATIONS

» What are your beliefs about learning, professional learning communities, students, your role in transforming your school, and others' role? Some call these beliefs core values or assumptions. Record them in your journal.
  • Be thoughtful and reflective.
  • Write until you are clear.
  • Be sure your statements are sentences.
  • Avoid jargon and platitudes.

» What goals do you have for yourself as a coach or for the school or organization you serve? What is your own theory of change and logic model for those goals? What becomes clearer to you when you develop a theory of change and logic model?

» What strategies would help ensure that you exemplify your values through coaching? What will you do to model your values or assumptions? What body, language, and emotional coherence will help in your effort? Think about the strategies you will use and record them on your calendar if necessary.

» Research theory of change, logic models, and Innovation Configurations to strengthen your ability to design these tools.

» Coach a principal or leadership team in building a theory of change, logic model, and KASAB chart for an effort they see as essential for their school community. Help them develop strategies to engage the entire staff in this work. With the principal and school leadership team, ask:
  • Is the theory aligned with what we know about learning and organizational change?
  • What readings and learning do you need to better understand organizational change and adult learning?
  • Is your current theory of change achieving the outcomes you want?
  • What other theories of change might better help your school reach its vision, mission, values, and goals?
  • Do current structures motivate and energize those in the organization?
  • What sanctions does the system use? With whom? When and for what? What celebrations and rewards are used?

STRATEGIES AND INVESTIGATIONS

- What strategies do you use so that people eagerly, authentically engage in change processes?
- What are the results of these strategies?
- What does your language of change suggest about collaboration? Goals? Values? Vision? Accountability? Learning?
- How does this show up with students?

Ask them to reflect with you about the value of these processes.

» Reflect on the value of coaching principals and school communities to build a shared vision and to clarify the team's expectations toward achieving the school's goals.

RESOURCES FOR CHAPTER 10

Killion, J. & Roy, P. (2009). *Becoming a learning school.* Oxford, OH: National Staff Development Council.

Munger, L. & von Frank, V. (2010). *Change, lead, succeed.* Oxford, OH: National Staff Development Council.

Easton, L. (Ed.). (2008). *Powerful designs for professional learning* (2nd ed.). Oxford, OH: National Staff Development Council.

"It is no longer enough to be smart — all the technological tools in the world add meaning and value only if they enhance our core values, the deepest part of our heart. Acquiring knowledge is no guarantee of practical, useful application. Wisdom implies a mature integration of appropriate knowledge, a seasoned ability to filter the inessential from the essential."

— Childre & Rozman, 2002

When I was a small child, I spent many hours with my grandparents. My mom worked, and after school we often found our way up the block for an afternoon visit and a snack in the comfort of my grandmother's loving home. My grandmother was gentle, funny, and loving, and I always wanted to be with her. I remember her quiet nature and her penetrating, twinkling eyes, but I also still can feel her hand holding mine — long, thin fingers, soft like warm clouds. I sat near her on the bed and watched her hands as she quilted. What patience! What persistence! What artistry! I watched her hands as she shelled peas and fried chicken, and I watched her hands as she made gardenia corsages, picked vegetables from her garden, and cared for all around her. All my growing up years until she died, what I really wanted was for her to do what she did so often, to hold my hand in hers. There was comfort there, love, and energy. I wonder if wisdom is like those hands — quiet, compassionate, warm, and loving — lifting up those held by them.

Wisdom has to do with our ways of making decisions in times of greatest complexity. Character is who we are. We think of Ghandi as wise because he chose nonviolence to change the world. He might have had an ethical character, but we do not focus on that; we focus on his wisdom. Some might say the same of Winston Churchill. At times his character may have been questionable, but his wisdom saved England.

Coaches who are most successful focus not only on developing their character and skills, but also on wisdom. Wisdom and developing wisdom may seem like an enigma. Some may even believe that wisdom comes with age and experience. Jo Anne O'Brian-Levin, author of *Business Revolution Through Ancestral Wisdom* (Outskirts Press, 2008), says that wisdom comes from seeking clarity in our lives, beliefs, relationships, and values, living with integrity, and continuously seeking access to our inner compass. Those who work to develop in these areas develop wisdom.

In my definition, a person is wise if she has extensive factual and theoretical knowledge, knows how to live well, is successful at living well, and gives hope to others through the model she is. Wise coaches know themselves, live in lightness, and are clear that they are on a lifelong learning journey of service to others. Was my grandmother wise by this definition? I think so. What did she teach me that helps me coach?

Acceptance. She accepted others as they were. Though she had high expectations for her children and grandchildren, she loved and enjoyed us just the way we were. Wise coaches see those they are coaching as wonderful human beings — gifts to the planet — who are working to make their way through the world. The wise coach takes pleasure in the presence of the individual being coached and the opportunity to engage in conversations that reshape lives — the life of the coach and of the leader.

Service. My grandmother's hands were for serving others. In her later years, when she had to live in a nursing home, she began to support a young nurse who was taking care of her. She helped get clothes for the nurse's family, counseled the young woman on parenting, and helped her deal with other life issues. Grandmother believed that as long as she was alive, she was here to serve. Coaches have a core belief that they are servants to those they coach. They empathize without sympathizing, and they find quiet, humble ways to lead those they coach to be strong, make thoughtful decisions for themselves, to model what they want to see in the world, and to lead others effectively. The wise coach does not demand or need attention or recognition for his or her contribution, but celebrates the leader's learning and successes. The wise coach gives the leader all the credit and finds joy simply serving others.

Self-awareness. My grandmother chose not to learn to drive and did not care much for TV. She knew who she was and held deep core values about life, family, community, church, and country. Coaches have a strong sense of who they are. They align their words, actions, and deeds with their values. They remain grounded in past experiences and yet seize opportunities to learn and grow themselves. Self-awareness is central to emotional intelligence; emotional intelligence is vital to successful leadership.

Persistence. My grandfather taught me to drive, but my grandmother was in the car calming and reassuring my siblings, who screamed, "She's going to kill us!" I learned to drive confidently because my grandmother celebrated my progress and cheered me on. She coached me not to be distracted by others and to concentrate on my goal. Wise coaches work diligently with others, never giving up on them, cheering them on. Many of leaders' challenges are long-term without simple solutions. Leaders working to raise student achievement in a low-performing school often face staff who may be resigned or resentful, who seldom collaborate; a lack of rigor in the curriculum and instructional plans; students who have low opinions of themselves as learners; parents disconnected from school; and teachers who may be under the threat of losing their jobs. Each of these factors affects the principal's ability to succeed and the

ASSUMPTIONS

» Wise coaches see themselves as servant coaches.

» Those with the deepest wisdom have clarity about who they really are, the problems they face, and what they really need.

» Wise coaches live in authenticity and transparency, and are content to enjoy the world around them.

» Those with great wisdom understand that integrity comes from a place of wholeness. Otherwise, we lack focus and power, and our energy is scattered.

» Wise coaches are eager to coach in a way that leads others to live well.

» Those with deep wisdom capitalize on their inner compass to direct and guide them toward their goals over the long term.

achievement of every child in that school. Highly effective coaches challenge leaders to work through issues with optimism, integrity, and perseverance and are the calming presence that guides the leader to confidence.

Transparency. Wise coaches are self-aware and live their core values in such a way that others never question them. No matter what I did, I could predict what my grandmother would think about it. That transparency in living was often a line in the sand for me — it guided my decision making. Would my grandmother approve of my doing this? Would she be proud? Coaches who are most effective live in transparency and authenticity. Those they coach count on them, trust their future to them, and grow strong and confident in their presence.

Lightness. I can never forget the joy in my grandmother's life and the light in her eyes. She loved a joke or a funny story and laughed often. Coaches cannot coach with negative energy. Cheerfulness and warmth spread most easily. Wise coaches spread positive emotions; they move people by articulating a dream that elicits optimism and energy. Neurologically, laughter instantly interlocks the limbic system. People who relish each other's company laugh easily and often when they are together. Wise coaches help others live in lightness.

Hope. One of my favorite stories is by Ron Suskind, *A Hope in the Unseen* (Broadway Books, 1998), about a young man named Cedric. Cedric was an inner-city high school student in Washington, D.C. Cedric wanted to succeed in school and the world, but he was challenged every day. He walked in unsafe neighborhoods, students in his school had little value for education, and the school environment was not conducive to learning. And yet Cedric had a powerful, wise teacher in his life. This teacher coached him in mathematics even when Cedric was not his student, helped the youth apply to colleges, and helped him seek financial aid. The teacher coached Cedric through many personal challenges as well. With this help, Cedric was accepted to Brown University. This teacher gave Cedric hope. Wise coaches lead others to set audacious goals for themselves and to have the confidence to achieve them.

Perhaps wisdom cannot be taught, but it certainly must be learned. How do we grow wiser as we learn to coach? How can we coach others to develop the wisdom essential to lead high-achieving schools? The questions are not whether we can learn to be wise in our interactions with others and in developing a compelling vision for the education of all children. The question is whether we have the will.

Coach well. When we are in service to others, we learn more about ourselves, we expand our understanding of human nature and the human condition, we have the ability to grow in empathy. When we live in lightness, we help others find joy. Just like my grandmother's beautiful hands, we comfort the angry, the challenged, the frustrated, the resigned, and the resentful. Through coaching, just like those hands, we bring comfort, optimism, and most importantly, audacious hope.

REFLECTIONS

Who in your life has been a model for you of wisdom? What impact did your models have on your personal journey toward wisdom?

What do you think is the value of coaches developing greater and greater wisdom?

Assess your strengths and challenges in the seven insights of wisdom discussed in this chapter.

STRATEGIES AND INVESTIGATIONS

» Take each of the insights of wisdom and make notes about your own strengths and challenges in those areas. Be thoughtful about what you might do to deepen your wisdom in areas of greatest challenge to you. Establish a challenging goal for yourself, a theory of change, and a logic model to help you achieve your goal.

Insight	Strengths	Challenges
Acceptance		
Service		
Awareness		
Persistence		
Transparency		
Lightness		
Hope		

» Reflect regularly in your journal about your progress. Share your insights with fellow coaches.

» Establish a place in your journal for building humor. Several times each day, search for the humor around you. Practice laughing every day! Reflect on shifts in your thinking, attitudes, and health.

» Enter in your journal times when you are not accepting of those around you. What is the impact of that lack of acceptance on your relationship with others? What doors have you closed for yourself?

The effective coach's self-assessment and goal-setting tool

STEP 1: Self-assessment.

Using the Innovation Configuration, note your skills in each of the desired outcomes. Do not just check a box. Identify where you are on the Innovation Configuration, state the level, and write your justification for your rating.

Desired outcome I: The coach builds a safe and nurturing environment in which those being coached are comfortable sharing work challenges, establishing strategies for building shared vision in their schools, and implementing purposeful innovations.

Level 1	Level 2	Level 3	Level 4	Level 5
The coach is a trusted confidante of the coachee.	The coach is trusted by the coachee.	Though the coach talks about the importance of trust in the relationship, the coachee is not comfortable being open and honest in coaching sessions.	The coach assumes trust in the relationship but does not intentionally focus on building a trusting relationship with the coachee.	The coach violates trust and places the coachee at risk.
The coach has high regard for the coachee's emotional safety and security.	The coach is conscious of being a model for the coachee and skillfully prepares for coaching sessions to ensure the coachee maintains a sense of wellness.	The coach understands and uses skills with the coachee that reflect adult learning styles; however, the coach has little understanding of a theory of change that would guide the learner to new leadership skills.	Coaching sessions are activity- and incident-driven, and focus on problem solving. Little emphasis is placed on learning new skills, developing new attitudes, or exploring the coachee's deeply rooted assumptions that may be holding him or her back.	The coach is more concerned about his or her own well-being and sees coaching as a way to increase his or her own confidence, power, and financial security.
The coach is conscious of his or her own intentions, and the coachee sees congruence between verbal and nonverbal cues.	The coach understands that all adults have unique learning styles and designs coaching sessions to best meet the coachee's needs.			The coach often lets his or her personal concerns and personal stories enter into the conversation during coaching sessions.
The coach has a deep understanding of individual and organizational change and is grounded in the principles of systems thinking and adult learning.	The coach has achieved success as a school leader and systems thinker.			
The coach maintains a high regard for the coachee at all times. Both coach and coachee are clear about their own values, philosophies, emotional and social well-being, and spirituality.	The coach has the coachee's best interests in mind at all times.			

Desired outcome II: The coach structures the learning to ensure that leaders develop knowledge and skills to create and lead learning communities in which all students and staff are learning.

Level 1	Level 2	Level 3	Level 4	Level 5
The coach uses a variety of modeling, mediating, visioning, and inquiry strategies to help the coachee understand communities, their dynamics and interactions, and their need for purpose and learning. The coach skillfully selects learning strategies and goal-setting systems that best meet the coachee's needs. The coach is grounded in the definition, standards, principles, and practices of professional learning.	The coach uses research and inquiry skills to help the coachee understand the characteristics of a professional learning community. The coach focuses the coachee on learning new skills, new attitudes, and new behaviors so that he or she is open to new possibilities and sets meaningful, challenging goals.	The coach uses questioning strategies skillfully in working with the coachee. The coach helps the coachee communicate and clarify goals and personal expectations but struggles to model or design effective learning strategies for the coachee.	The coach uses storytelling and questioning strategies that leave the coachee dwelling on issues and blaming others for the situation. The coach, unclear about the characteristics of a professional learning community, uses incident-focused problem-solving strategies that do not build vision.	The coach listens to the coachee's stories but is unclear when to interject questions that might lead to learning. The coach is not familiar with the characteristics of a professional learning community, leaving the coachee to take whatever direction seems best at the time.

Desired outcome III: The coach continuously learns in order to improve.

Level 1	Level 2	Level 3	Level 4	Level 5
The coach routinely self-assesses and regularly learns new and effective strategies for coaching. The coach works collaboratively with other coaches to strengthen his or her skills and to reflect on the impact coaching is having. The coach regularly sets goals for himself or herself to use new skills and strategies. He or she seeks a coach to facilitate his or her learning and to monitor his or her own progress. The coach consistently uses the coachee's feedback about coaching's effect on the coachee's learning. The coach modifies his or her approach based on that learning.	The coach is continuously learning new and effective strategies for coaching principals. The coach regularly discusses with other coaches what they are learning and experiencing. The coach regularly sets personal goals to increase his or her effectiveness. The coach seeks the coachee's feedback about his or her effectiveness in developing the coachee's competence to lead professional learning communities.	The coach attends conferences and sessions on becoming an effective coach and stays current in the thinking, skills, and research around coaching principals. The coach rarely discusses with others what the coach is learning. The coach rarely if ever sets goals for himself or herself to increase his or her effectiveness. The coach seeks feedback from coachees about his or her effectiveness.	The coach views himself or herself as a learner, but is confident she or he has effective strategies for coaching principals. The coach seeks general feedback from the coachee but rarely seeks sufficient or precise feedback in order to identify specific strengths and weaknesses in his or her coaching work that can help guide a learning plan.	The coach is confident in his or her coaching and relies on past learning to hone the coachee's skills.

STEP 2: Determine strengths and weaknesses.

Synthesize your key thoughts as you review your notes and evidence of your comments.

My strengths:

_____

_____

_____

My weaknesses:

_____

_____

_____

STEP 3: Establish a goal.

What goal is essential for you to increase your effectiveness as a coach? Challenge yourself.

What will it look like when you have achieved your goal? What new skills, attitudes, and dispositions will you have? What new behaviors will you develop? What new results would you expect from those you coach?

What goal is essential for me to set for my own learning? What is my rationale?		
What new skills, attitudes, dispositions, and behaviors will I develop? What will I be doing differently than I am doing now?	What impact will this have on those I coach?	What aspirations do I have for myself?

STEP 4: Determine a plan of action.

Consider what it will it take to achieve the goal. Be sure to consider what has prevented you from achieving goals in the past.

How will you overcome those breakdowns in your learning?

_____
_____
_____
_____
_____
_____
_____
_____

What must you do differently?

_____
_____
_____
_____
_____
_____
_____
_____

List the steps you must take.

_____
_____
_____
_____
_____
_____
_____
_____

STEP 5: Sequence the actions.

Be thoughtful in developing your logic model.

Challenging, results-oriented goal	Long-term outcomes	Intermediate goals	Short-term goals	Essential resources	Inputs
Measures of effectiveness					
Artifacts					

Assets that I have that will facilitate my learning:

_____

_____

_____

_____

Barriers that I will face:

_____

_____

_____

_____

Strategies I will use to overcome those barriers:

_____

_____

_____

_____

Strategies I will use to monitor my progress:

_____

_____

_____

_____

Artifacts I will gather that will reflect my learning:

_____

_____

_____

_____

Philosophy of coaching

The values that guide my actions in coaching others:
- I care greatly about my coachee's success. I will do whatever it takes to listen well, to be thoughtful about my questions, and to learn aggressively how to coach well.
- I will treat the coachee with respect at all times. I will keep my coachee's confidence. I will build trust by being reliable.
- I will focus on developing my coachee's competence and confidence to lead; both are significantly important to being respected by others.
- I will listen from the coachee's point of view. I know I have experiences that shaped my leadership, but my experiences are not my coachee's experiences, my solutions not his solutions.

My beliefs about learning:
- Learning means changing behavior.
- Learning is energizing and a powerful force in a leader's success in complex times and within complex organizations.
- Learning is collaborative and organic; the more I work with others, the faster and better I learn.

My purpose in coaching principals:
I want to watch school leaders grow and learn so that more children in our community and nation are skilled, confident, and ready for the challenges they will face when they leave K-12 education.

My hopes and aspirations for those I coach:
I hope that they develop the skills, attitudes, dispositions, and behaviors essential to lead communities where all are learning aggressively.

The things I need to learn to be more effective as a coach:
- To listen well and ask strategic questions.
- To develop the wisdom and thoughtfulness to lead others to discover who they are, what they are learning, and the power they have to shape their futures and the futures of others.

Establish your own philosophy of coaching

The values that guide my actions in coaching others:

_____

_____

_____

_____

My beliefs about learning:

_____

_____

_____

_____

My purpose in coaching principals:

_____

_____

_____

_____

My hopes and aspirations for those I coach:

_____

_____

_____

_____

The things I need to learn to be more effective as a coach:

_____

_____

_____

_____

A protocol for designing protocols

One skill coaches need is the ability to help others create protocols that lead to new learning. This strategy helps coaches and facilitators design their own protocols.

STEP 1: Establish the purpose for the protocol.
- To examine text.
- To examine adult work.
- To engage in problem solving.
- To reflect on practice.

STEP 2: Define the outcome.
Declare the outcome that is expected at the end of the protocol. Is it to think differently, to look at different points of view, to compare and contrast solutions, to gain commitment, to determine future actions?

STEP 3: Describe the work to be done.
- What activities or strategies are essential for the outcome to be achieved?
- Will participants watch videotapes of teachers teaching?
- Are they going to better define a problem the school is experiencing as a result of student behavior?
- Are they going to share big ideas from the text they have been reading?

STEP 4: Sequence the learning activities and determine a time frame for each.

STEP 5: Pilot the protocol. Afterward, reflect with the team on its effectiveness in producing the desired result.

STEP 6: Make changes based on feedback.

Step 7: Use it!

Sample protocol

The scenario

The leader you have been coaching has been working with teachers to integrate new writing strategies in their classrooms. Several teachers have been early adopters, and their use of the suggested strategies has resulted in dramatic increases in not only students' love for writing but the quality of their work. These teachers are excited and are proud of themselves and their students.

STEP 1: Establish the purpose.

With the principal, begin to ask thoughtful questions about shifts at the school. The principal says he really wishes he could share the ideas that have worked so well for the early adopters, their new skills, the new teaching strategies, and the results in student work. You suggest creating a protocol for teachers to share what they are learning. The principal wants the whole staff to examine these teachers' work and to reflect on how others might begin using similar strategies in their classrooms.

STEP 2: Define the outcome.

The principal begins to explore the outcomes. Since the purpose has been set as examining teacher work, the principal begins to articulate the goals or outcomes of the protocol: "When the teaching staff leaves the protocol, I want them to leave with one new strategy they will try with their students and to leave confident that the strategy will have a positive effect on their students' writing.

STEP 3: Describe the work to be done.

The principal begins to describe the strategies he wishes to use during the session(s). You and he explore many possibilities. Finally, he decides that the teachers' lessons will be videotaped, focusing on effective instructional strategies. He determines the best ways to encourage teachers' willingness to be videotaped. He also wants teachers to look at actual student work, so he modifies his original outcome to examine both adult and student work. He decides to ask the early adopters to select student work that best exemplifies before-and-after snapshots of improvement. He and the teachers involved will talk about what this will look like. The principal then wants small groups to read the student papers and, using the district's scoring rubric, to reflect on the differences before and after the teachers' use of the new instructional strategies. Next, the principal wants the teams to show their videotapes and lead the group through a discussion of their observations about instructional strategies. They will have to chart individually and then in a group the critical attributes of the new approaches. Finally, after defining the critical attributes, each team will select a strategy to try in the classroom to start teachers' new learning journey in teaching writing effectively. The principal seems pleased with his ideas.

STEP 4: Sequence the learning activities and determine a time frame.

The principal establishes a timeline for these strategies. He realizes that, before using the protocol, he will visit with the early adopters, get permission to tape their lessons, ask for them to select an array of papers with distinctive before-and-after results. He also will ask one teacher to facilitate the protocol during the afternoon session.

He establishes a plan to share the idea with the entire faculty and requests that a few experience the protocol prior to the entire faculty using it so that he can get feedback about timing, pace, and strategy effectiveness. Then he specifies the time allotted to each activity.

The protocol

1. The facilitator shares that the purpose of the work today is to identify an essential instructional strategy that participants are willing to incorporate into lesson plans and teaching for the next week and the strategies for the day. *(5 minutes)*

2. The facilitator asks each teacher to read the six pieces of student writing and make notes about the similarities and differences in the papers from the same student. *(15 minutes)*

3. The facilitator asks a volunteer at each table to lead discussion and a recorder to make notes of the table group's common observations. *(15 minutes)*

4. The early adopter team shares videos of its lessons and asks observers to record the critical attributes of those lessons that they believe contributed to the shifts in the student work that they read. *(15 minutes)*

5. Table groups describe the critical attributes of the instructional strategies and determine which approaches they will use in their classrooms. *(15 minutes)*

6. Each team shares what strategies and assistance teachers will need from the early adopters to apply the strategies well and their expectations for their students. *(10 minutes)*

7. The facilitator leads conversations with the entire group about the protocol's effectiveness. *(5 minutes)*

STEP 5: Pilot the protocol.
The principal agrees that the best way to determine the timing and pace of the session is to pilot the protocol with a small group before using it with the whole staff. The design requires more time than a typical afternoon staff meeting, so he will use the protocol during the next early dismissal. Realizing the need for follow-through, the principal decides to repeat the protocol several times. He envisions breaking the protocol into two sessions to give teachers time to think and to ask questions.

STEP 6 : Make changes based on feedback.
The principal knows that the outcome is the essential component and that the protocol may be revised many times before participants make authentic changes in their instructional practices that lead to greater student learning.

STEP 7: Use the protocol.
The principal may use other protocols in addition to look at writing from different angles, but he is ready to use this one regularly to help teaching teams examine their work, their success in adopting new strategies, and their impact on student learning and achievement.

A protocol for establishing norms

1. Clarify the value and purpose of norms in creating effective collaboration. *(5 minutes)*

2. Ask that the team determine the major breakdowns members observe in their work with others. Chart the comments. *(15 minutes)*

3. Establish norms based on the breakdowns others are experiencing. *(15 minutes)*

4. Ensure that everyone is in consensus about the norms and willing to use them in collaborative sessions. *(10 minutes)*

5. Remind everyone that the protocols will be posted at each session and reviewed before the agenda begins. Also remind the group that at each session, the team will reflect on members' use of the protocols to determine whether the team is having fewer breakdowns and if new norms are needed. *(5 minutes)*

6. Reflect with the group about the process. *(5 minutes)*

A protocol for structured feedback sessions with other coaches

1. Establish the purpose of the session, i.e. to strengthen skills in asking questions, to develop listening skills, to assist leaders in establishing new practices. *(5 minutes)*

2. Ask that participating coaches review their goals, progress, and challenges they are facing. Be sure to have each participant share his or her portfolio. *(10 minutes)*

3. Each participant asks thoughtful questions that will help the speaker reflect on his or her own learning and shift the work to achieve his or her goals. *(10 minutes)*

4. Practice coaching with each other in triads. Teams may generate hypothetical leaders or use issues that are arising with leaders as long as confidentiality is not violated. *(30 minutes)*

5. Reflect on the coaching sessions. What went well? What challenges did we face? What new ideas or strategies might we use that would have strengthened the coaching experience for the leaders and produced different results? *(15 minutes)*

6. Share readings and research in the field of coaching. The facilitator of the session may choose a protocol that facilitates teams analyzing text. *(15 minutes)*

LEARNING FORWARD'S
Standards for Professional Learning

Learning Communities: Professional learning that increases educator effectiveness and results for all students occurs within learning communities committed to continuous improvement, collective responsibility, and goal alignment.

Leadership: Professional learning that increases educator effectiveness and results for all students requires skillful leaders who develop capacity, advocate, and create support systems for professional learning.

Resources: Professional learning that increases educator effectiveness and results for all students requires prioritizing, monitoring, and coordinating resources for educator learning.

Data: Professional learning that increases educator effectiveness and results for all students uses a variety of sources and types of student, educator, and system data to plan, assess, and evaluate professional learning.

Learning Designs: Professional learning that increases educator effectiveness and results for all students integrates theories, research, and models of human learning to achieve its intended outcomes.

Implementation: Professional learning that increases educator effectiveness and results for all students applies research on change and sustains support for implementation of professional learning for long-term change.

Outcomes: Professional learning that increases educator effectiveness and results for all students aligns its outcomes with educator performance and student curriculum standards.

Source: Learning Forward. (2011). *Standards for Professional Learning.* Oxford, OH: Author.

Austin Parks & Recreation. (n.d.). *Treaty Oak history.* Available at www.ci.austin.tx.us/treatyoak/hist1.htm.

Beslin, R. & Reddin, C. (2006, January-February). Trust in your organization's future: Building trust inside and out is a key part of the communicator's role as corporate conscience. *Communication World, 23*(1), 29-32.

Blanchard, K., Meyer, P.J., & Ruhe, D. (2007). *Know can do!* San Francisco: Berrett-Koehler Publishers.

Bloom, B. (1986, February). Automaticity: "The hands and feet of genius." *Education Leadership, 43*(5), 70-77.

Bloom, G., Castagna, C., Moir, E., & Warren, B. (2005). *Blended coaching: Skills and strategies to support principal development.* Thousand Oaks, CA: Corwin Press.

Brookfield, S.D. (1991). The development of critical reflection in adulthood. *New Education, 13*(1), 39-48.

Bureau of Labor Statistics. (n.d.). *Occupational outlook handbook, 2010-11 edition.* Available online at www.bls.gov/oco/ocos007.htm.

Childre, D. & Rozman, D. (2002). *Overcoming emotional chaos.* San Diego, CA: Jodere Group.

Churchill, W. (1940, June 4). *Speech before the House of Commons.* Available at http://history.hanover.edu/courses/excerpts/111chur.html.

Cornett, J. & Knight, J. (2008). Research on coaching. In J. Knight (Ed.), *Coaching: Approaches and perspectives.* Thousand Oaks, CA: Corwin Press.

Costa, A. (2008). *The school as a home for the mind: Creating mindful curriculum, instruction, and dialogue.* Thousand Oaks, CA: Corwin Press.

Costa, A. & Garmston, R. (2002). *Cognitive coaching: A foundation for renaissance schools.* Norwood, MA: Christopher-Gordon.

Covey, S.M.R. (2008). *The speed of trust.* New York: Free Press.

Deal, T. & Peterson, K. (1998). *Shaping school culture: The heart of leadership.* San Francisco: Jossey-Bass.

Dess, N.K. (2001, July 1). *The new body-mind connection.* Available at www.psychologytoday.com/articles/200107/the-new-body-mind-connection.

Far West Laboratory. (1984). *Making our schools more effective: Proceedings of three state conferences.* San Francisco: Author.

Fullan, M. (2001). *Leading in a culture of change.* San Francisco: Jossey-Bass.

Fullan, M. (2008). *The six secrets of change: What the best leaders do to help their organizations survive and thrive.* San Francisco: Jossey-Bass.

Gates, S.M., Ringel, J.S., Santibanez, L., Ross, K.E., & Chung, C.H. (2003, June). *Who is leading our schools? An overview of school administrators and their careers.* Santa Monica, CA: RAND.

Gladwell, M. (2008). *Outliers.* New York: Little, Brown, and Company.

Glasser, W. (1998). *Choice theory: A new psychology of personal freedom.* New York: HarperCollins.

Goleman, D. (1995). *Emotional intelligence.* New York: Bantam Books.

Goleman, D. (1998). *Working with emotional intelligence.* New York: Bantam Books.

Goleman, D. (2002). *Primal leadership: Realizing the power of emotional intelligence.* Boston: Harvard Business School Press.

Goleman, D. (2006). *Social intelligence: The new science of human relationships.* New York: Bantam Books.

Grant, A.M., Curtaynes, L., & Burton, G. (2009, September). Executive coaching enhances goal attainment, resilience and workplace well-being: A randomised controlled study. *The Journal of Positive Psychology, 4*(5), 396-407.

Hall, L.M. (2000). *Secrets of personal mastery: Advanced techniques for accessing your highest levels of consciousness.* New York: Crown Publishing Group.

Hall, G.E. & Hord, S.M. (2010). *Implementing change: Patterns, principles, and potholes* (3rd ed.). Upper Saddle River, NJ: Allyn & Bacon.

Hargrove, R. (1995). *Masterful coaching: Extraordinary results by impacting people and the way they think and work together.* San Francisco: Jossey-Bass.

Hart, L.A. (1983). *Human brain and human learning.* White Plains, NY: Longman Publishing.

Hirsh, S. & Killion, J. (2007). *The learning educator.* Oxford, OH: NSDC.

Hoffer, E. (2008). *Reflections on the human condition.* Titusville, NJ: Hopewell Publications.

Hord, S., Rutherford, W., Huling-Austin, L., & Hall, G. (1987). *Taking charge of change.* Alexandria, VA: ASCD.

Hord, S. & Sommers, B. (2008). *Leading professional learning communities: Voices from research and practice.* Thousand Oaks, CA: Corwin Press.

Knowles, M.S. (1973). *The adult learner: A neglected species.* Houston, TX: Gulf Publishing.

Knowles, M.S. (1975). *Self-directed learning: A guide for learners and teachers.* Englewood Cliffs, NJ: Prentice Hall/Cambridge.

Knowles, M.S. (1984). *Andragogy in action: Applying modern principles of adult learning.* San Francisco: Jossey-Bass.

Knowles, M.S. (1989). *The making of an adult educator.* San Francisco: Jossey-Bass.

Knowles, M.S. (1990). *The adult learner: A neglected species.* Houston, TX: Gulf Publishing.

Kofman, F. & Senge, P.M. (1995). Communities of commitment: The heart of learning organizations. In S. Chawla & J. Renesch (Eds.), *Learning organizations: Developing cultures for tomorrow's workplace.* Portland, OR: Productivity Press.

Institute for Educational Leadership. (2000, October). *Leadership for student learning: Reinventing the principalship.* Washington, DC: Author.

Learning Forward. (2011). *Standards for Professional Learning.* Oxford, OH: Author.

Leithwood, K., Louis, K.S., Anderson, S., & Wahlstrom, K. (2004). *How leadership influences student learning.* Available at www.wallacefoundation.org/ KnowledgeCenter/KnowledgeTopics/CurrentAreasofFocus/EducationLeadership/ Pages/HowLeadershipInfluencesStudentLearning.aspx.

Leonard, G. (1991). *Mastery: The keys to success and long-term fulfillment.* New York: Penguin Books.

Levey, J. & Levey, M. (1998). *Living in balance.* New York: MJF Books.

Marzano, R.J. & Waters, T. (2009). *District leadership that works.* Bloomington, IN: Solution Tree.

Marzano, R.J., Waters, T., & McNulty, B.A. (2005). *School leadership that works.* Alexandria, VA: ASCD.

Merriam, S.B. & Caffarella, R.S. (1999). *Learning in adulthood.* San Francisco: Jossey-Bass.

Moen, F., Skaalvik, E., & Hacker, C.M. (2009). Performance psychology among business executives in an achievement-oriented environment. *Journal of Excellence,* (13), 78-96.

National Association of Elementary School Principals. (2008). *Leading learning communities: Standards for what principals should know and be able to do* (2nd ed.). Alexandria, VA: Author.

O'Brian-Levin, J.A. (2008) *Business revolution through ancestral wisdom.* Parker, CO: Outskirts Press.

Ohio Leadership Advisory Council. (2008). *Ohio's leadership development framework.* Available online at www.ohioleadership.org/up_doc/70532ODEOLAC.pdf.

Olalla, J. (2003a). *The observers we are: Coaching for professional and personal mastery.* Unpublished work.

Olalla, J. (2003b). *Trust.* Olney, MD: Newfield Network.

Olalla, J. (2000). *Speech acts I: Distinctions and assertions.* Unpublished work.

Pert, C.B. (1997). *Molecules of emotion.* New York: Scribner.

Peterson, K.D. (1982). Making sense of principals' work. *The Australian Administrator, 3*(3).

Peterson, K.D. (1998, May). Realities and reform: Living with the daily realities of principals' work. *Instructional Leader, (11)*3.

Reeves, D.B. (2009). *Leading change in your school, How to conquer myths, build commitment, and get results.* Alexandria, VA: ASCD.

Reiss, K. (2007). *Leadership coaching for educators: Bringing out the best in school administration.* Thousand Oaks, CA: Corwin Press.

Resnick, L. (n.d.). *Principles of learning.* Pittsburgh, PA: Institute of Learning, University of Pittsburgh. Available at http://ifl.lrdc.pitt.edu/ifl/index.php/resources/principles_of_learning.

Rock, D. (2006). *Quiet leadership: Six steps to transforming performance at work.* New York: HarperCollins.

Rock, D. & Page, L.J. (2009). *Coaching with the brain in mind: Foundations for practice.* Hoboken, NJ: John Wiley & Sons.

Rolls, J. (1995). The transformational leader: The wellspring of the learning organization. In S. Chawla & J. Renesch (Eds.), *Learning organizations: Developing cultures for tomorrow's workplace,* pp. 101-109. Portland, OR: Productivity Press.

Senge, P.M. (1994). *The fifth discipline: The art & practice of the learning organization.* New York: Doubleday.

Sparks, D. (2002). *Designing powerful professional development for teachers and principals.* Oxford, OH: NSDC.

Sparks, D. (2007). *Leading for results* (2nd ed.). Thousand Oaks, CA: Corwin Press & NSDC.

Sparks, D. (2010). *Leadership 180.* Bloomington, IN: Solution Tree.

Spiegel, E. (2011). *Why seeing (the unexpected) is often not believing.* Available at www.npr.org/2011/06/20/137086464/why-seeing-the-unexpected-is-often-not-believing.

Stoltzfus, T. (2008). *Coaching questions: A coach's guide to powerful asking skills.* Virginia Beach, VA: Vcoach22.

Suskind, R. (1998). *A hope in the unseen.* New York: Broadway Books.

Tice, L.E. (1989). *A better world, a better you: The proven Lou Tice "Investment in Excellence" program.* Upper Saddle River, NJ: Prentice Hall.

Tschannen-Moran, M. (2004). *Trust matters: Leadership for successful schools.* San Francisco: Jossey-Bass.

Waters, T., Marzano, R.J., & McNulty, B.A. (2003). *Balanced leadership: What 30 years of research tells us about the effect of leadership on student achievement.* Aurora, CO: Mid-continent Research for Education and Learning.

Kay Psencik at the Treaty Oak in Austin, Texas.

About the author

Kay Psencik is a senior consultant for Learning Forward. She has coached teachers, principals, and district leaders in schools throughout the United States and around the world.

Psencik earned a bachelor of arts degree from the University of Mary Hardin Baylor, a master's degree in educational administration from Southwest Texas State University, and a doctorate in educational administration from Baylor University. She served as a public educator for more than 30 years and retired from Texas public schools in 1999, when she began consulting with schools and districts. She specializes in assisting in strategic planning, helping schools develop professional learning communities, and facilitating teams of teachers developing standards-driven curriculum, assessment, and instructional plans.

She has published articles and two previous books: *Accelerating Student and Staff Learning: Purposeful Curriculum Collaboration* (Corwin Press, 2009) and *Transforming Schools Through Powerful Planning* (NSDC, 2004), co-authored with Stephanie Hirsh.

NOTES

NOTES

NOTES